Techno

DAVID BOYLE and
MARGARET WILSON MARTIN

TEACHER
TIMESAVERS

Published by Scholastic Ltd,
Villiers House,
Clarendon Avenue,
Leamington Spa,
Warwickshire CV32 5PR
1 2 3 4 5 6 7 8 9   6 7 8 9 0 1 2 3 4 5
© 1996 Scholastic Ltd
Text © 1996 David Boyle and Margaret Wilson Martin

Author David Boyle and Margaret Wilson Martin
Editor Irene Goodacre
Assistant editor Libby Weaver
Series designer Joy White
Designers Claire Belcher
Illustrations Liz Thomas
Cover illustration Frances Lloyd
Cover photograph Martyn Chillmaid
Scottish 5–14 links Sue Ellis
Northern Ireland links Trisha Kell

Designed using Aldus Pagemaker
Printed in Great Britain by Clays Ltd, St Ives plc

British Library Cataloguing-in-Publication Data
A catalogue record for this book is
available from the British Library.
ISBN 0-590-53455-6

Contents

About the authors

David Boyle is a teacher adviser for design and technology. Margaret Wilson Martin is a first-school technology co-ordinator.

What is design and technology?

Design and technology is essentially a creative activity which involves children in:
- recognising and responding to needs, opportunities and challenges;
- considering and evaluating possible solutions;
- selecting one of these options;
- planning, modelling and making a product to meet an identified need;
- evaluating and possibly modifying the product.

The revised National Curriculum Orders for design and technology recognise three types of activity:
- Design and make assignments (DMA) – holistic activities involving children in the whole creative process. These are often suggested in the notes (pages 7–12) which offer guidance on the photocopiable sheets.
- Focused practical tasks – where children are involved in learning a particular skill, technique or aspect of knowledge or understanding. These are not necessarily creative, but essential if children are to learn and progress.
- Investigating, Disassembling and Evaluating Activities (IDEAs) – where children investigate an existing product to inform their own design decisions.

The photocopiable sheets in this book have been drawn up to include all three types of activity, and to provide opportunities to cover the programmes of study for design and technology at both Key Stages 1 and 2.

The activities are divided into three main sections – Getting it together, Making it work and Record keeping.

Vocabulary

At the end of each set of practical tasks are some photocopiable sheets to develop or reinforce the technological vocabulary required.

Assessment

Each section also features a number of tasks designed specifically for assessment purposes. These are presented as open-ended technology challenges.

Health and safety

The aim of this book is to save teacher time, but design and technology is a practical subject and there is no substitute for effective teacher input, not least in the area of the health and safety of the children. The section on skills and techniques (pages 5 and 6) should offer support in this area.

Uses of Information Technology

Opportunities for the use of IT are apparent throughout the book – reports can be processed, graphics software can be used for modelling ideas, data collected on spreadsheets or databases and control software used to control electrical devices.

Basic skills and techniques

Scissors skills

Encourage the children to cut out shapes carefully, pointing the scissors away from them, *and* the children they are sitting next to. Show them how to turn the card when they come to a corner and keep the scissors moving in the same direction. If necessary when they come to a difficult corner let them carry straight on and tidy it up afterwards.

Hole punch skills

Save any scrap card and let the children use it to practise using the hole punch. When they have had adequate practice show them how to remove the base of the hole punch and turn it upside down so that they can see exactly where the hole is going to be punched. Let them make some dots on the card and punch these out. They are now ready to punch pre-marked holes. Centrally marked holes are not accessible using a hole punch so you will need to show the children how to punch these out using a belt punch or a card drill. Alternatively use a sharp pencil with a blob of Plasticine or Blu-Tack underneath the marked hole.

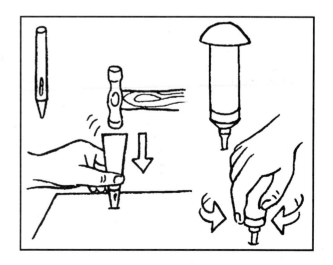

Scoring skills

Show the children how to score card using an old biro with a fine point or a magic cutter. They can then fold the card along the scored line.

Working with wood

Children should be shown how to secure timber in a vice or bench hook, and how to use a junior hacksaw to cut it out safely. Remind them that the saw will jam if they push down too hard.

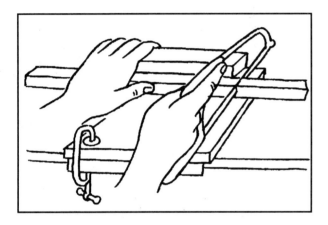

Making 3D corner joints

Cut out squares from paper or card and score both diagonals. Cut one diagonal into the middle, overlap two triangles and glue them together to form a corner joint (page 34).

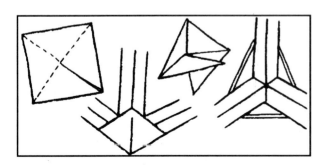

Sewing skills

- Threading a needle – this may take a bit of practice. Hold the needle upright and push one end of the thread through the hole, or eye.
- Tying a knot – thread your needle, then hold the end of the thread in your left hand between finger and thumb. Wind it twice loosely around your finger. Pass the needle under the loops from left to right. Slip the thread off your finger and pull tight.

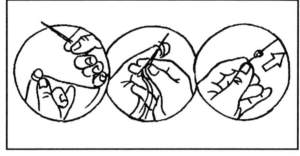

- Running stitch – push the needle up from underneath the fabric. Pull it through until you reach the knot. Push it down again a little further along. Keep on going up and down alternately.
- Backstitch – make one stitch and bring the needle up to start the next stitch, as for running stitch. Put the needle back into the fabric right by

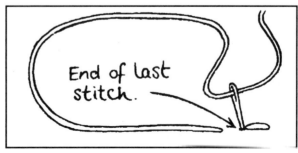

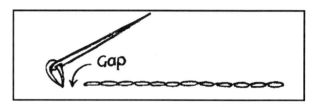

the end of the last stitch. Bring it up again further on. Make the gap the same size as one stitch. Put the needle in where the last stitch ended again. Go on like this.

- Sewing on a button – push the needle up through the fabric and through one of the holes in the button. Pass the needle down through the button's other hole, then through the fabric. Pull the thread tight until the button lies flat. Go back up through the first hole and repeat this several times. Finish off on the back of the fabric.
- Oversewing – hold the fabric flat and push

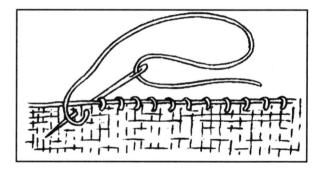

the needle through it from behind, so that it comes towards you. Pull the thread through. Take the needle back behind the fabric (so that the stitch loops over the edge of the fabric) to start the next stitch.

- Finishing off – do two or three stitches on top of each other, then cut the thread.

The photocopiable sheets

References to the PoS for Design and Technology in the National Curriculum for England and Wales are noted (in brackets) after each activity title. Links to the Scottish Guidelines and Northern Ireland Curriculum are included in separate tables on pages 13 and 14.

Getting it together

Paper and card

Car parts (KS1: 1b; 2a; 3c; 4b–d; 5a, f, g) offers practice in scissor skills, hole punch skills, gluing and with paper fastener joints.

The hungry caterpillar (KS1: 1b; 2a; 3b, e; 4a, b; 5f, g) again gives scope for hole punch practice. Suggested DMA – as an extension, use the hole punch and paper fasteners to make a simple hungry caterpillar puppet from circles of card about 10cm across.

Our Ted (KS1:1b; 2a; 3b, c, f; 4a–d, f; 5a, e–g) involves more hole punch practice, as well as an introduction to paper fastener joints and simple linkages.

Cedric the skeleton (KS1:1b; 2a; 3b, c, f; 4a–d, f; 5a, e–g, also calls for hole punch practice, as well as using paper fastener joints and simple linkages. Artstraws make effective bones if flattened and glued on.

Build a house (KS2: 1b; 2a–c; 4a–g; 5a, c, g, j, k) provides a net for a house which introduces scoring and folding. Suggested DMAs – how could you waterproof the roof of your house? Group your houses together in a village and add lights to them.

Four-wheel drive (KS2: 1b; 2a–c; 4a–g; 5a, c, g, j, k) gives practice in more advanced cutting, scoring and folding skills. Suggested DMA – fit your body shell on to a construction kit base and motorise your vehicle.

Today's weather and **Weather wheel** (KS1: 1b; 2a; 3b–d, f; 4a–f; 5a, d–g) ask children to cut a window and use a simple paper fastener linkage to attach a background wheel. Suggested DMA – design a rotary mechanism like this to tell a story, such as the life cycle of the frog.

Net for a cube (KS2: 1b; 2a–c; 4a–g; 5a, c, g, j, k) again uses cutting and scoring skills. Suggested DMA – design an identicube by showing information on the different faces of the cube, such as name, address, family, hobbies, pets, favourites. Make a mobile from the class's cubes.

Artstraws

Joining Artstraws: 1 (KS2: 1a, b; 2a–c; 3a–g; 4a–g; 5a–c, e, g–k) shows some simple techniques for joining Artstraws together. Challenge pupils to use Artstraws to make a temporary shelter for equipment on a lunar expedition. Remind them that it must be light and strong.

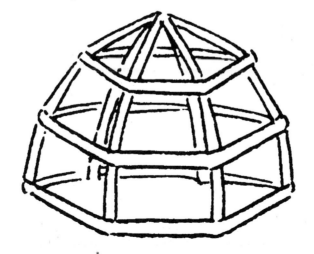

Joining Artstraws: 2 (KS2: 1a, b; 2a–c; 3a–g; 4a–g; 5a–c, e, g–k) offers more advanced techniques. Children could try making a land yacht with solid paper sticks held together with elastic bands or pvc tubing, bead wheels, and a sail made from plastic sheet.

Joining Artstraws: 3 (KS2: 1a, b; 2a–c; 3a–g; 4a–g; 5a–c, e, g–k) provides practice in making simple moving joints and using them for model making.

Joining Artstraws: 4 (KS2: 1a, b; 2a–c; 3a–g; 4a–g; 5a, b, e, g–k) shows how to make wattle and daub panels using simple timber frames, woven Artstraws and papier mâché or plaster.

Skinny Stan the Artstraw Man (KS2: 1b; 2a, b; 4a–g; 5a–d, g–k) creates a model man by threading and joining Artstraws. Suggested DMA – make a Skinny Stan puppet.

Timber

Home Sweet Home (KS1: 1a, b; 2a, b; 3c–f; 4a–f; 5d–g) gives a simple introduction to measuring and cutting square section wood to make a timber collage. Suggested DMA – ask the children to design their own timber collage pictures. Plan this out first using flattened Artstraws.

Viking Houses: 1 (KS2: 1a, b; 2a–c; 3a–g; 4a–g; 5a, b, e, g–k) and **2** (KS2: 1a, b; 2a–c; 3a–g; 4a–g; 4a–g; 5, b, e, g–k) provides a plan for a simple triangular prism framework to make a Viking house.

Techniques for joining wood (KS2: 1a, b; 2a–c; 3a–g; 5a, b, e, g–k) provide a range of ideas for joining square section timber and dowel.

2D corner joints – a sheet of pre-marked corner triangles for copying on to thin card and cutting out.

3D corner joints – a sheet of pre-marked corner triangles for copying on to thin card and cutting out.

Food

Safety and hygiene (KS1: 1b; 2c; 3a, b, e; 4a, e; 5e–g; KS2: 1a, b; 2a–c; 3a–g; 4a–g; 5a, b, g–k) gives children advice on the basic hygiene precautions they should observe when working with food.

Fresh fruit salad (KS2: 1a, b; 2a–c; 3a–g; 4a–g; 5a, b, g–k) offers an opportunity to investigate, cut and prepare fruits. Encourage pupils to make good use of colour and think about presentation.

Tropical taster (KS1: 1a, b; 2a–c; 3a–c, e, f; 4a, e, f; 5d–g; KS2: 1a, b; 2a–c; 3a–g; 4a–g; 5a, b, g–k) lets pupils use and mix fruit juices and soft drinks to design a children's cocktail. Hold a tasting session to judge which drink looks, and tastes, most appealing. As an extension or follow-up, ask the children to design a new milk shake.

Iced biscuits (KS2: 1a, b; 2a–c; 3a–g; 4a–g; 5a, b, g–k) provides a simple biscuit recipe. Children should think carefully about shapes and the colours and flavours they wish to use for decoration.

Fancy sandwiches (KS2: 1a, b; 2a–c; 3a–g; 4a–g; 5a, b, g–k) is a competition to design a sandwich, using different breads and fillings, and thinking about texture, appearance and labelling.

Pizza (KS2: 1a, b; 2a–c; 3a–g; 4a–g; 5a, b, g–k) gives a simple recipe for a pizza base. Use it as a starting point for a pizza challenge – children can try and test various toppings, choose their favourite combination and give it a name.

Textiles

Button it! (KS1: 1b; 2a; 3c, e, f; 4c–f; 5d–g; KS2: 1a, b; 2a–c; 3a–g; 4a–g; 5a, b, e, g–k) is a sheet which gives practice in the skill of sewing on buttons.

Teddy's bed (KS1: 1a, b; 2a–c; 3a–f; 4a–f; 5d–g; KS2: 1a, b; 2a–c; 3a–g; 4a–g; 5a, b, e, g–k)

gives instructions on making a card bed. As an extension, children could design and add a headboard. Encourage them to think of different shapes and possible techniques (such as attaching matchsticks to wood).

Ready for bed (KS1: 1a, b; 2a–c; 3a–f; 4a–f; 5d–g; KS2: 1a, b; 2a–c; 3a–g; 4a–g; 5a, b, e, g–k) provides simple ideas for a quilt cover and pillow for the card bed made with the previous sheet. Children should be encouraged to come up with ideas for decorating the bed linen with fabric and trimmings.

Pot-pourri bag (KS1: 1a, b; 2a–c; 3a–f; 4a–f; 5d–g; KS2: 1a, b; 2a–c; 3a–g; 4a–g; 5a, b, e, g–k) shows how to construct a simple bag with a tie.

Sam the scarecrow (KS1: 1a, b; 2a–c; 3a–f; 4a–f; 5d–g; KS2: 1a, b; 2a–c; 3a–g; 4a–g; 5a, b, e, g–k) is a fabric collage idea for younger children. It gives practice in cutting and gluing both natural and man-made materials.

Fred bear (KS1: 1b; 2a; 3c; 4a–f; 5d–g; KS2: 1a, b; 2a–c; 3a–g; 4a–g; 5a, b, e, g–k) is a lacing and threading exercise for younger children. Pupils could colour in Fred's face or sew on buttons for eyes, and stick on felt for his mouth and nose. (A collar of masking tape around the end of your ribbon or wool will make it easier to thread.)

Clara the caterpillar (KS1: 1b; 2a; 3c; 4a–f; 5d–g; KS2: 1a, b; 2a–c; 3a–g; 4a–g; 5a, b, e, g–k) shows the children how to use a paper pattern to work with felt or Vivelle.

Construction kits

The playground (KS1: 1a–c; 2a, c; 3a–f; 4a–f; 5a–g; KS2: 1a, b; 2a–c; 3a–g; 4a–g; 5a–e, g–k) challenges pupils to build an item of equipment for a playground. This activity is aimed at KS1 children.

The fairground (KS2: 1a, b; 2a–c; 3a–g; 4a–g; 5a–e, g–k) asks for a thrill ride design, incorporating motors or air power – this is more suitable at KS2 level.

Malleable materials

Working with dough (KS1: 1a, b; 2a–c; 3a–f; 4a–f; 5d–g) introduces skills and techniques for using materials such as Plasticine, play dough or clay.

Structures

Barney the bull (KS2: 1a, b; 2a–c; 3a–g; 4a–g; 5a, b, e, g–k) gives some ideas for making simple frame structures.

Frame it! (KS2: 1a, b; 2a–c; 3a–g; 4a–g; 5a, b, e, g–k) shows how to make rigid frameworks by triangulation.

Strong beams (KS2: 1a, b; 2a–c; 3a–g; 4a–g; 5a, b, e, g–k) shows how the strength of card or paper can be increased by folding, rolling and corrugation. Challenge pupils to make a beam from one sheet of A4 paper – then see how many exercise books it will support.

Stability (KS2: 1a, b; 2a–c; 3a–g; 4a–g; 5a, b, e, g–k) investigates the use of larger and heavier bases to improve stability. Hold a competition to see who can make the tallest tower, using old newspaper and some method of joining such as elastic bands, paper clips or masking tape.

Reclaimed materials

Investigating cardboard boxes (KS1: 1a–c; 2a–c; 3a–f; 4a–f; 5a–g) shows how to disassemble and use old boxes. As an alternative, pupils could try turning their original box inside out, then sticking it back together, using masking tape to hold it in place while the adhesive dries. This will give a clean box for decoration or model making.

Corrugated card or plastics

Joining up (KS2: 1a, b; 2a–c; 3a–g; 4a–g; 5a–c, e, g–k) gives ideas for using these materials. The children should practise making these joins before they begin the main activity.

Vocabulary

Matching the names (KS1: 1b, c; 4a; 5a, c, f, g) is a simple vocabulary sheet for basic hand tools.
Using simple hand tools (KS1: 1b, c; 4a; 5a, c, f, g; KS2: 1b, c; 4a; 5j, k) can be used to record the names and uses of some simple tools. As the children become familiar with different hand tools, ask them to fill in this sheet.
Simple hand tools: wood, (KS1: 1b, c; 4a; 5a, c, f, g; KS2: 1b, c; 4a; 5j, k) **Simple hand tools: fabric,** (KS1: 1b, c; 4a; 5a, c, f, g; KS2: 1b, c; 4a; 5j, k) **Simple hand tools: food** (KS1: 1b, c; 4a; 5a, c, f g; KS2: 1b, c; 4a; 5j, k) ask children to label some basic tools. On the second and third sheets the labels should be (clockwise from top left):
• scissors, knitting needles and yarn, fabric crayons and fabric paint, crochet hooks, sewing machine, needles and pins, iron;
• rolling pin, sieve, whisks, cutters, funnel, mixing bowl, jug, spatula, baking tins.

Assessment

Greeting cards, (KS1: 1a–c; 2a–c; 3a–f; 4a–f; 5a, c–g; KS2: 1a–c; 2a–c; 3a–g; 4a–g; 5a–c, e, g–k)
Dick Whittington (KS2: 1a–c; 2a–c; 3a–g; 4a–g; 5a–c, e, g–k) and **Island life** (KS1: 1a–c; 2a–c; 3a–f; 4a–f; 5a–g; KS2: 1a–c; 2a–c; 3a–g; 4a–g; 5a–c, e, g–k) are all open-ended assessment sheets which can be used to assess aspects of children's design and technology capability as outlined in the Progress review sheet (page 141).

Making it work

Musical instruments

Sounds familiar is a recording sheet for identification of everyday sounds. Collect up to 20 objects that make different sounds, or put together or buy a sounds tape. Ask the children to guess the sounds and record their ideas on this sheet.
Blow it! (KS2: 1a–c; 2a–c; 3a–g; 4a–g; 5a, b, e–k) investigates making sounds by blowing, using Artstraws. Remind the children to throw away all the Artstraws they have used at the end of the activity.
Shake it all about! (KS2: 1a–c; 2a–c; 3a–g; 4a–g; 5a, b, e–k) is an activity about making sounds by shaking.
Join in with the band! (KS2: 1a–c; 2a–c; 3a–g; 4a–g; 5a, b, e–k) gives some ideas on making sounds by plucking strings. Stress that care must be taken when stretching elastic bands.
Get with the beat (KS2: 1a–c; 2a–c; 3a–g; 4a–g; 5a, b, e–k) investigates percussion sounds.
Getting into a scrape (KS2: 1a–c; 2a–c; 3a–g; 4a–g; 5a, b, e–k) deals with sounds made by scraping.
Good vibrations! (KS2: 1a–c; 2a–c; 3a–g; 4a–g; 5a, b, e–k) investigates vibrations. Suggested IDEA – investigate a collection of musical instruments from home and abroad and discuss how they work.

Paper engineering

Windmill net: 1 and **2** (KS1: 1b; 2a, b, 4a–f; 5a, b, d–g) provide an exercise in cutting, scoring and making hole punch and paper fastener joints. Pupils should copy or trace the nets on to card.

Castle pop-up (KS2: 1a, b; 2a–c; 3a–g; 4a–g; 5a–c, e, g–k) is a simple, but effective, box section pop-up idea.
Haunted castle (KS2: 1a, b; 2a–c; 3a–g; 4a–g; 5a–c, e, g–k) gives practice in cutting and scoring to make hinges. Younger children may need help to start cutting the windows, alternatively they could glue window-shaped hinged flaps over the top of the existing windows.
It's magic (KS1: 1a–c; 2a–c; 3a–f; 4a–f; 5a, c–g) provides a simple Artstraw sliding mechanism. Once children have completed the rabbit in the hat, encourage them to use an Artstraw slider to make another pop-up model.
Time on your hands (KS1: 1a–c; 2a–c; 3a–f; 4a–f; 5a, c–g) contains a clock face with rotating hands, a simple rotary mechanism. This is a useful aid for learning to tell the time. Challenge pupils to use the same mechanism to make a 'machine' for leaving messages for the milkman or to develop any ideas of their own.
Life goes sliding by (KS2: 1a, b; 2a–c; 3a–g; 4a–g; 5a–c, e, g–k) is a card slit with sliding mechanism. Children may need help to start cutting the slit, alternatively they could fold it over and use scissors to start the cut. Encourage them to devise their own scenes and to use them to tell stories.
Pop-up (KS1: 1a–c; 2a–c; 3a–f; 4a–f; 5a, c–g) shows how to use a box section for a simple pop-up mechanism. Suggest that pupils try using several different-sized box sections to create a 3-D effect.
Captain Quack (KS2: 1a, b; 2a–c; 3a–g; 4a–g; 5a–c, e, g–k) provides an activity in cutting, scoring and folding to make an opening mouth. Pupils could use this technique to make a full crew for Captain Quack's ship.

V-fold surprise (KS2: 1a, b; 2a–c; 3a–g; 4a–g; 5a–c, e, g–k) investigates use of the V-fold mechanism.

Windy weather: 1 and **2** (KS1: 1b; 2a; 3a–f; 4a–f; 5a, c–g) provide ideas for using simple linkages. Ask the children to create other pictures, using the same idea.

Wheels and axles

Wheely good ideas (KS1: 1a, b; 2a, b; 3a–f; 4a–f; 5a, b, d–g; KS2: 1a, b; 2a–c; 3a–g; 4a–g; 5a–c, e–k) offers a range of ideas for inexpensive wheels and fittings. Encourage the children to try out as many wheels as they can and to compare their performance.

Making a chassis (KS1: 1a, b; 2a, b; 3a–f; 4a–f; 5a, b, d–g; KS2: 1a, 2b; 2a–c; 3a–g; 4a–g; 5a–c, e–k) again provides a range of ideas for chassis construction. Why not arrange the children into six groups and ask one group to make each kind of chassis? Have a race to find the best one.

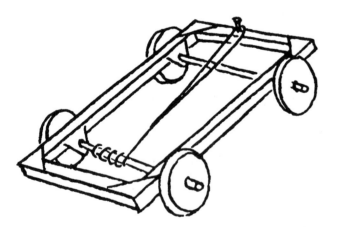

Movement in water

Floaters and sinkers (KS1: 1b; 2a–c) is a recording sheet which children can use when sorting objects into groups according to whether they float or sink.

Making boats (KS1: 1b; 2a–c; 3a–f; 4a–f; 5b, d–g; KS2: 1a, b; 2a–c; 3a–g; 4a–g; 5a–k) offers a number of ideas for boat construction. Divide the class into 'design teams' and allocate each group one card. After the race suggest that children try adding weights to their boats, to see which takes longest to sink. Results could be recorded on page 86.

Movement in air

Make a spinner (KS2: 1a–c; 2a–c; 3a–g; 4a–g; 5a–c, f–k) provides a template for a simple spinner with suggestions for further investigations.

Leonardo da Vinci's parachute (KS2: 1a–c; 2a–c; 3a–g; 4a–g; 5a–c, f–k) gives children a net with suggested investigations. As an extension or follow-up they could find out more about the life and work of da Vinci.

Hinges

Hinges (KS1: 1a,b; 2a–c; 3a–f; 4a–f; 5a–g; KS2: 1a–c; 2a–c; 3a–g; 4a–g; 5a–c, e, g–k) lists a range of ideas for simple hinges. Challenge pupils to use one of the methods to make a jointed animal, or a door to a secret cave.

Levers

Introducing levers (KS2: 1a–c; 2a–c; 3a–g; 4a–g; 5a–c, e–k) provides information about levers and lever words. Suggested IDEA – encourage pupils to make a class collection of levers.

Investigating levers (KS2: 1a–c; 2a–c; 3a–g; 4a–g; 5a–c, e–k) offers simple ideas about balance.

Advise the children, when making their mobiles, to start from the bottom and work up, using Blu-Tack to keep the threads in place until it is balanced.

Linkages

Dino-jaws (KS1: 1a, b; 2a, c; 3a–f; 4a–f; 5a, c–g) is a template for a dinosaur with an opening mouth which uses a simple single arm linkage.

Wavy Ted (KS1: 1a, b; 2a, c; 3a–f; 4a–f; 5a, c–g) is a template for a teddy with a moving arm worked by a simple single arm linkage.

Ear Ear (KS2: 1a, b; 2a–c; 4a–g; 5b, c, g–k) is a template for a rabbit with moving ears, this time using a simple double arm linkage.

Moo-ve it! (KS2: 1a, b; 2a–c; 4a–g; 5b, c, g–k) is a template for a cow with moving legs which uses a simple double arm linkage (parallel movement).

Cocky Locky (KS2: 1a, b; 2a–c; 4a–g; 5b, c, g–k) is a template for a chicken's head with opening beak, using a double arm linkage (alternating movement).

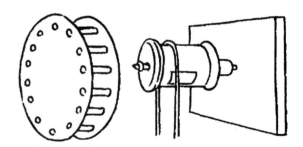

Pulleys

Pulley investigations (KS2: 1a–c; 2a–c; 3a–g; 4a–g; 5a–k) helps pupils to find out about how pulleys work. Two simple ideas for home-made pulleys are shown above.

The Iron Man (KS2: 1a–c; 2a–c; 3a–g; 4a–g; 5a–k) suggests some stimulus ideas to make simple working models which use pulleys.

Conveyors and tracked vehicles (KS2: 1a–c; 2a–c; 3a–g; 4a–g; 5a–k) provides stimulus ideas for working models.

Using a motor (KS2: 1a–c; 2a–c; 3a–g; 4a–g; 5a–k) explains the use of pulleys in gearing down a motor and offers simple ideas for motorised models.

Gears

Investigations on gears (KS2: 1a, b; 2a–c; 5c, g–k) provides further help in finding out about gears.

Using gears (KS2: 1a–c; 2a–c; 3a–g; 4a–g; 5c, f–k) shows how to use construction kit gears and offers simple ideas about gearing up and down.

Name the gear (KS2: 1a–c; 2a–c; 3a–g; 4a–g; 5a–k) lays out the different types of gear and their uses.

Making your own gears (KS2: 1a–c; 2a–c; 3a–g; 4a–g; 5a–k) gives a range of ideas for making gears from inexpensive materials.

Aztec calendar: 1 provides background information on the Aztec calendar outline provided on page 107.

Aztec calendar: 2 (KS2: 1b; 2a–c; 4a–g; 5a–c, g–k) gives the template for the construction of a working Aztec calendar. One full turn of each wheel represents one month. Turn the solar calendar 18 times for one year. Where is the sacred calendar positioned? Only after 52 years on the solar calendar (52 x 18 = 936 turns) will they both be back at their starting point. Discuss the gear principle behind this model.

Pneumatics and hydraulics

Using balloons (KS1: 1a, b; 2a–c; 3a–f; 4a–f; 5a, c–g, illustrates some simple ideas for balloon-powered pneumatic models using an old detergent bottle as a balloon pump.

Using syringes (KS2: 1a–c; 2a–c; 3a–g; 4a–g; 5a–c, e–k), demonstrates the use of tubing and disposable syringes to make pneumatically-operated models. Never use syringes that have been used for injections, and be aware that a large syringe can push out a smaller one with great force.

Hydraulics (KS2: 1a–c; 2a–c; 3a–g; 4a–g; 5a–c, e–k) shows the use of tubing and disposable syringes to make hydraulically-operated models. Don't forget that water-filled syringes make ideal water pistols! You have to be able to trust your children! This method, however, has the advantage that water is not compressible so the movement is far more positive than that in a pneumatic system.

Cams and cranks

Cammy the Duck (KS2: 1b; 2a–c; 4a–g; 5a–c, g–k) provides a template for a nodding duck operated by a simple cam system. This can be tricky and is therefore suitable for the most able children.

Cranky the cheeky clown (KS2: 1b, 2a–c; 4a–g; 5a–c, g–k) is a template for a clown with a tongue that sticks out operated by a simple crank mechanism.

Magnets

Furry Ferdinand (KS1: 1a, b; 2a–c; 3a–f; 4a–f; 5b, d–g; KS2: 1b; 2a–c; 4a–g; 5a–c, g–k) offers some simple investigations with magnets, using iron filings to give facial hair to a face drawn in a tray. The tray helps to prevent the filings scattering. Pupils could improve Ferdinand's disguise by adding a hat or glasses cut from thin card with a paper clip taped on.

Island boat race (KS1: 1a, b; 2a–c; 3a–f; 4a–f; 5b, d–g; KS2: 1b; 2a–c; 4a–g; 5a–c, g–k) provides some simple investigations with magnets where paper clips are moved underneath a sheet of card. Suggested DMA – design your own magnetic toy or game.

Electricity

Electrical toys and games (KS2: 1a–c; 2a–c; 3a–g; 4a–g; 5a–k) has some stimulus ideas for making electrically operated toys. Before you begin, make sure the children have a basic understanding of electricity, including circuits and switches.

Investigating a torch (KS2: 1b, c; 2a–c; 5a, c, d, f–k) gives an introduction to exploded diagrams.

Vocabulary

Technology toolbox (KS2: 1b; 5k) is a word search based on the names of basic hand tools.

Technology jumblies (KS2: 1b; 5k) asks children to solve some anagrams of technology words (mechanisms).

Assessment

Adventure World, **Castaway** and **Crossing the island** (KS2: 1a–c; 2a–c; 3a–g; 4a–g; 5a–k) are all open-ended assessment sheets.

Record keeping

Planning sheets

PLANIT sheet is a graphical planning sheet which uses the acronym PLANIT to remind staff of the main aspects of the planning procedure. This could be enlarged to A3 to permit more information to be shown.

Planning sheet is an optical aid to developing focused activities.

Planning for assessment shows how the programme of study statements can be used for everyday teacher assessment and to inform future planning (see below).

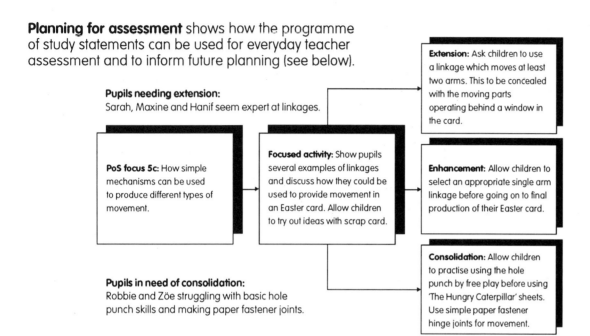

Pupils needing extension:
Sarah, Maxine and Hanif seem expert at linkages.

PoS focus 5c: How simple mechanisms can be used to produce different types of movement.

Focused activity: Show pupils several examples of linkages and discuss how they could be used to provide movement in an Easter card. Allow children to try out ideas with scrap card.

Extension: Ask children to use a linkage which moves at least two arms. This to be concealed with the moving parts operating behind a window in the card.

Enhancement: Allow children to select an appropriate single arm linkage before going on to final production of their Easter card.

Consolidation: Allow children to practise using the hole punch by free play before using 'The Hungry Caterpillar' sheets. Use simple paper fastener hinge joints for movement.

Pupils in need of consolidation:
Robbie and Zöe struggling with basic hole punch skills and making paper fastener joints.

Graphics

3D drawings (KS2: 1b; 3d, e; 5k) is designed to give children practice in representing solid boxes in 2D drawings. They can also use isometric paper (see page 132) as a guide. Once they have mastered this drawing technique, introduce the idea of **crating**, which involves simplifying complex drawings by representing their component parts as simple boxes.

Shading and texture (KS2: 1b; 3d, e; 5k) shows how to enhance design drawings by using shading and texture to represent different materials.

Light and shadow (KS2: 1b; 3d, e; 5k) offers shading practice with light coming from a chosen direction. Full light, partial shade and heavy shadow could be indicated.

One point perspective (KS2: 1b; 3d, e; 5k) shows how to add realism to design drawings by the use of simple perspective. Encourage pupils to try drawing hollow boxes on the back of the sheet. Remind them that practice makes perfect!

Two point perspective (KS2: 1b; 3d, e; 5k) adds further realism to graphical representation by the use of two point perspective. Suggestions for further practice are included.

Three pages of **grids** provide guidelines for sketching and lettering. Large squares, small squares and an isometric grid. Small pieces of Blu-Tack can be used to keep the grid in place underneath the working sheet.

Children's design sheets

Design and technology project (KS2: 1a; 3a–g) these pages, put together, make an A5 folded booklet for recording the process of design work for older children. The booklet takes pupils through the design process, from points to consider when designing, through to a final evaluation of the finished product.

Keeping evidence

Evidence sample sheet is a blank sheet to keep a photographic or illustrated record of children's products. This will enable samples to be kept as part of a standards bank and will be particularly useful where children have undertaken construction kit work, or where completed projects have been taken home.

Disassembly/evaluation

IDEAs sheet: 1 is a simple recording sheet for IDEAs, ideal for Key Stage 1 work.
IDEAs sheet: 2 (KS2: 1c; 3a; 5f–k) forms an A5 folded booklet to record IDEAs. It could be enlarged to an A4 folded booklet, if required, to allow more space for information and diagrams.
Progress review sheet is a suggested record sheet to be kept in a pupil's school record file or record of achievement. This could be updated on an annual basis and would facilitate reporting to parents on children's design and technology capability.

Technology resources needed is a useful blank appeal sheet for consumables which can be taken home to parents. Suggested DMA – involve children in designing appeal sheets, letters or posters for additional consumable items. These are much more likely to reach their intended audience.

Design and Technology Award recognises pupil achievement in aspects of design and technology.

Parental permission letter for food activities is self-explanatory, but is an essential part of preparation for any food activities.

Links to Scottish 5–14 Guidelines

This book will help teachers to address the following knowledge and understanding outcomes of *Environmental Studies 5–14*:
Technology: Understanding and Using the Design Process
Health: Healthy and Safe Living
Science: Understanding Energy and Forces

Each section of activities develops key features of the above knowledge and understanding outcomes. This is indicated in the list below, along with the stages (P1–3, P4–6 or P7–S2) for which each section is broadly appropriate. Key teaching points for each activity are detailed on pages 7–14.

Teachers will also be able to see how the activities and follow-up work may be organised and presented to contribute to outcomes in Information Technology and the 5–14 Guidelines for Language and Mathematics.

Technology

Practical skills, techniques and safe procedures; Properties of materials and tools in relation to their practical use
P1–3: Paper and card; Textiles; Malleable materials; Reclaimed materials; Musical instruments
P1–3 and P4–6: Construction kits; Vocabulary (Getting it together); Paper engineering; Linkages
P4–6: Artstraws; Timber; Structures; Corrugated card or plastics; Wheels and axles; Hinges

Design and manufacturing processes; Selecting and using design processes
P1–3 and P4–6: Assessment (Getting it together); Paper engineering
P4–6: Movement in water; Movement in air; Electricity; Assessment (Making it work); Graphics; Children's design sheets; Keeping evidence; Disassembly/evaluation

Devices and tools associated with control and their applications
P1–3 and P4–6: Linkages
P4–6: Levers; Pulleys; Gears; Pneumatics and hydraulics; Cams and cranks

---

Health Education

Health and safety in the environment
P1–3 and P4–6: Food

Science

Forms and sources of energy; Properties and uses of energy
P4–6: Musical instruments; Movement in water; Movement in air

Forces and their effects
P4–6: Movement in water; Movement in air; Pneumatics and hydraulics; Magnets

Northern Ireland Curriculum – Science and Technology (Proposals)

Many of the activities in this book will support the technology content of the Programme of Study for Levels 1–5 of AT2 – Knowledge and Understanding of Science and Technology. Some suitable sections are suggested below.

	1	2	3	4	5
Forces and Energy	Explore forces which push, pull or make things move. Listen to and identify sources of sound in their immediate environment. Find out that light comes from a variety of sources. Explore colour in the immediate environment. (Musical instruments; Movement in water)	Explore how pushes and pulls make things speed up or stop. Explore devices including toys which move e.g. wind up/battery toys or Roamer. (T) Produce movement in simple ways e.g. push/pull levers, model swing. (T) Explore ways of making sounds with familiar objects. Explore the use of light including colour in road safety. Know that electricity can be dangerous. (Paper and card; Artstraws; Paper engineering)	Find out about the range of energy sources in school and at home. Know about the safe use of mains electricity and its associated dangers. Investigate how sounds are produced when objects vibrate. Make instruments which produce sound e.g. shakers and drums. (T) Explore how light travels through some materials and not through others. (Musical instruments; Electricity)	Find out the sources of energy in a variety of models and machines. Make models which incorporate an energy source e.g. syringes and tubing to make a Jack in the box. (T) Investigate the formation of shadows. Construct simple circuits using components such as switches, bulbs and batteries. Investigate conductors and insulators. (Pneumatics and hydraulics; Electricity)	Understand the difference between renewable and non-renewable energy resources and the need for fuel economy. Investigate the effects of varying current in a circuit to make bulbs brighter or dimmer. Investigate the reflection of light from mirrors or other shiny surfaces. They incorporate an energy source into models which can be controlled. (T)
Materials	Work with a range of everyday materials in a variety of activities. Assemble and re-arrange materials e.g. construct using building blocks. (T) Sort a range of everyday objects into groups according to the materials from which they are made. (Paper and card; Textiles; Malleable materials)	Explore the properties of materials including shape, colour, texture and behaviour. Find out some everyday uses of materials. Explore different ways of joining materials e.g. using tags, string, fasteners, folds, stitches, adhesives or staples. (T) (Paper and card; Textiles; Reclaimed materials)	Investigate similarities and differences in materials and objects and sort them according to their properties. Choose appropriate materials and components when constructing. (T) Find out how human activities create a variety of waste products. (Construction kits; Paper engineering; Linkages)	Investigate the properties of materials and how these relate to their uses. Consider the properties of materials when planning and constructing working models. (T) Understand that some waste materials can be recycled and that this can be of benefit to the environment. (Artstraws; Timber; Structures; Wheels and axles; Hinges)	Investigate the distinctive properties of solids, liquids and gases as exemplified by water. Relate changes in state to the water cycle. Understand that when new materials are formed, change is permanent. Investigate how rusting can be controlled.

Car parts

✤ Copy or glue this page on to thin card.

✤ Colour the two sides of the car and cut them out carefully.

✤ Cut out four wheels. Fix them to the car parts with paper fasteners.

✤ Glue the two sides of your car on to a small box.

Wheels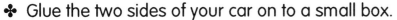

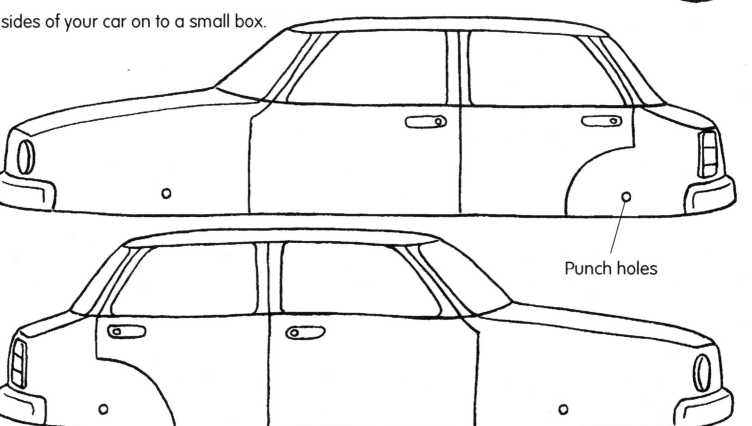

Punch holes

Paper and card

Name _____

The hungry caterpillar

✤ Cut out the leaf shapes.

✤ Punch some holes from these leaves for the hungry caterpillar to eat.

✤ The hungry caterpillar is getting full now. See if you can punch a few of the juicy parts (the darker patches) for him.

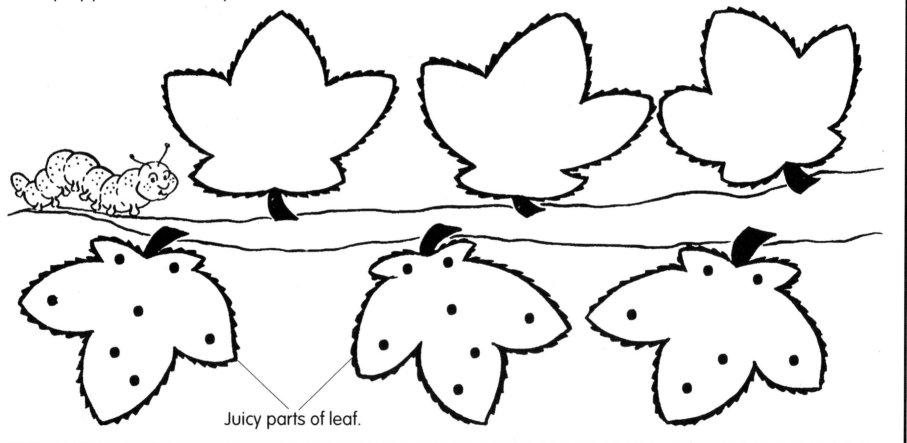

Juicy parts of leaf.

Our Ted

♣ Copy or glue teddy on to thin card.

♣ Colour him in and cut him out carefully.

♣ Punch holes where shown, then join him together with paper fasteners.

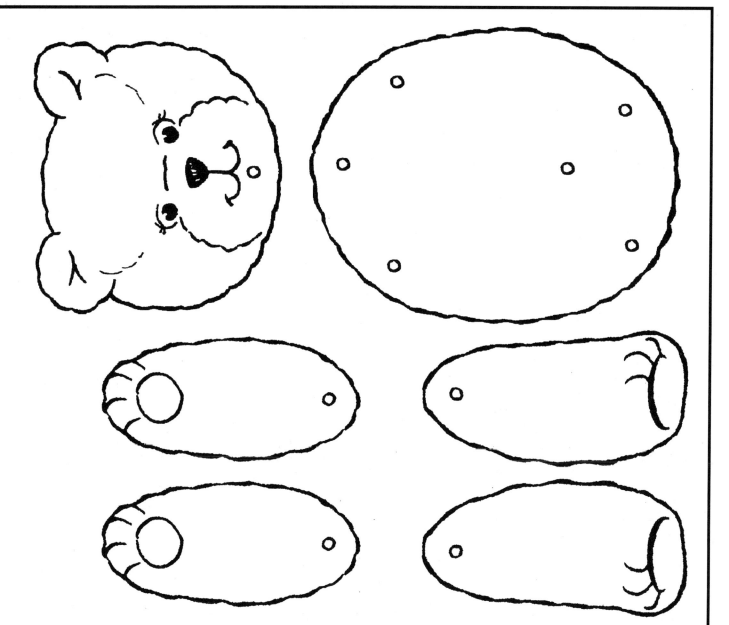

Name _____

Paper and card

Cedric the skeleton

♣ Copy or glue Cedric on to thin card.

♣ Cut his parts out carefully.

♣ Punch holes where shown.

♣ Join him together with paper fasteners.

♣ Glue on some flattened Artstraws for bones.

Build a house

✤ Copy or glue the house parts on to thin card.

✤ Cut carefully around the outlines of the shapes.

✤ Fold along the dotted lines.

✤ Glue the long flap to join your house together.

✤ Then stick the roof to the roof flaps.

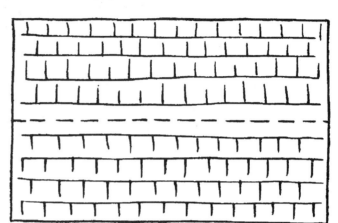

Name _____

Paper and card

Four-wheel drive

❖ Copy or glue the car shape on to thin card and colour it in.

❖ Cut it out and score along the dotted lines.

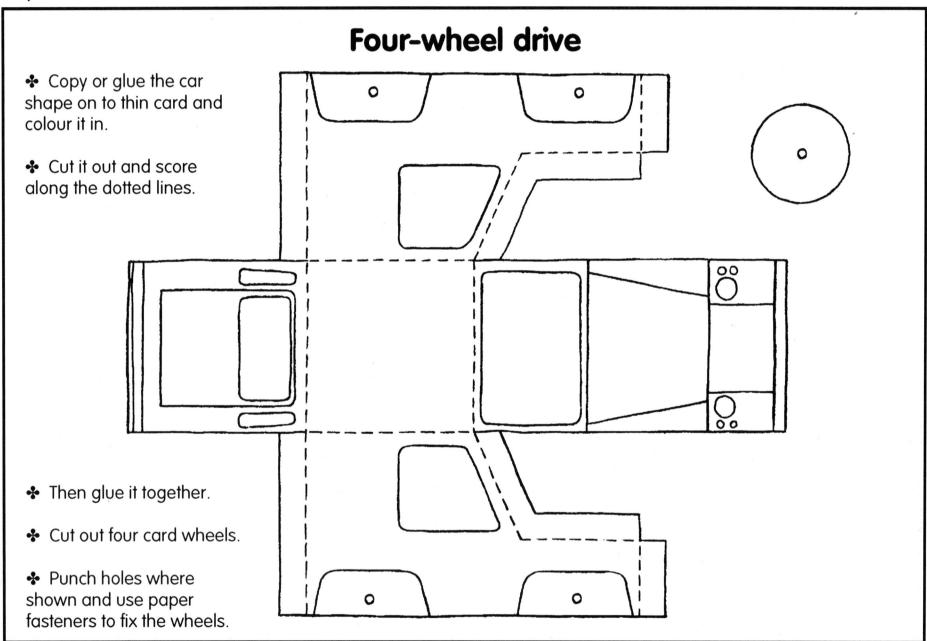

❖ Then glue it together.

❖ Cut out four card wheels.

❖ Punch holes where shown and use paper fasteners to fix the wheels.

Today's weather

❖ Copy or glue this television on to thin card.

❖ Punch a hole below to fix the weather wheel.

❖ Punch a hole in the middle of the circle so that you can cut it out.

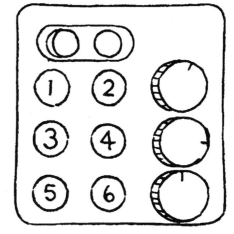

❖ Move on to the Weather wheel on page 22.

Paper and card

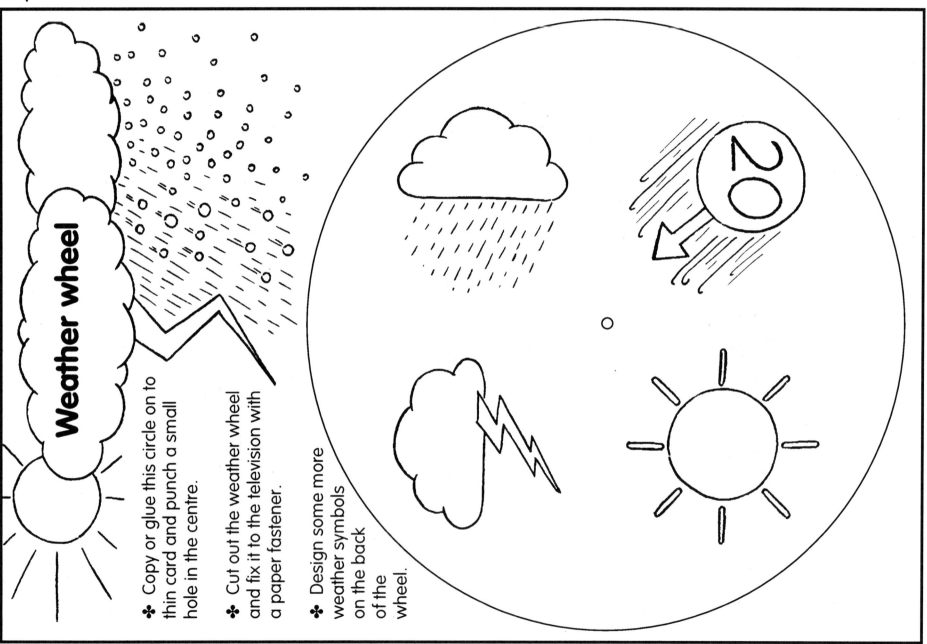

Weather wheel

✤ Copy or glue this circle on to thin card and punch a small hole in the centre.

✤ Cut out the weather wheel and fix it to the television with a paper fastener.

✤ Design some more weather symbols on the back of the wheel.

20

✤ Copy or glue this cube net on to thin card.

✤ Cut it out and glue it together to make the cube.

Net for a cube

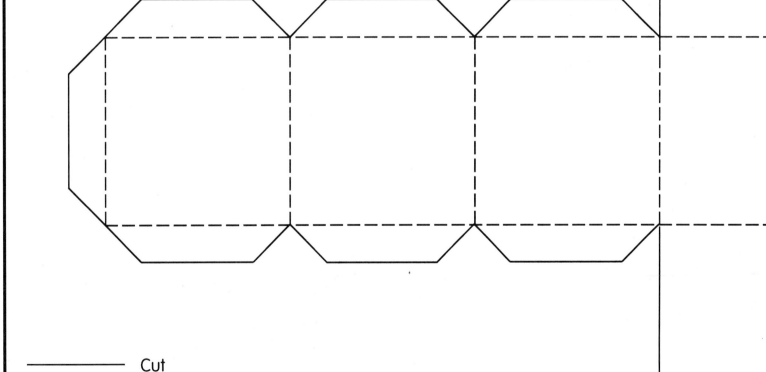

——————— Cut

– – – – – – Score

Name _____

Artstraws

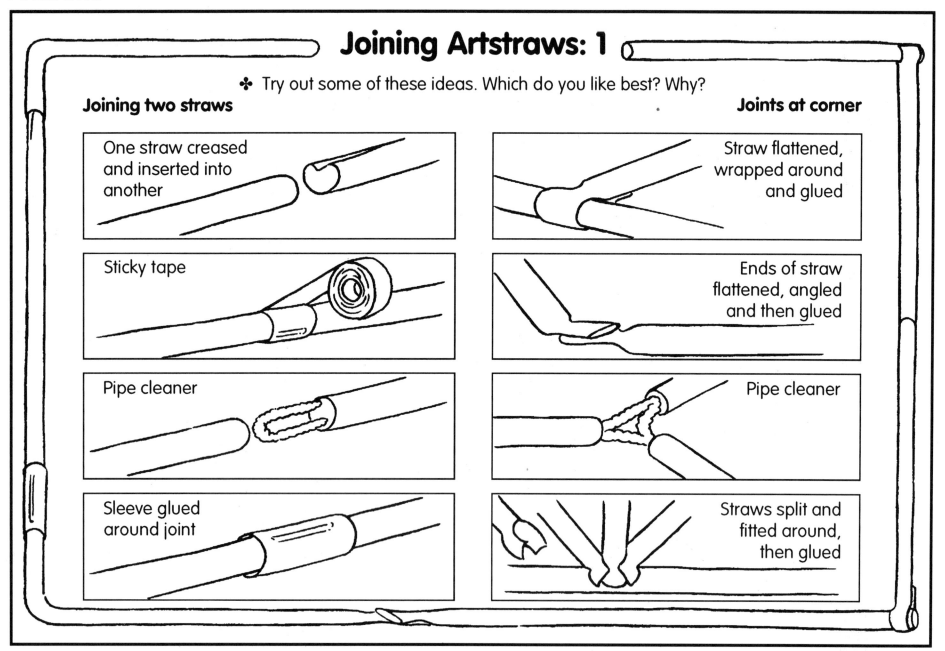

Joining Artstraws: 1

♣ Try out some of these ideas. Which do you like best? Why?

Joining two straws

One straw creased and inserted into another

Sticky tape

Pipe cleaner

Sleeve glued around joint

Joints at corner

Straw flattened, wrapped around and glued

Ends of straw flattened, angled and then glued

Pipe cleaner

Straws split and fitted around, then glued

Joining Artstraws: 2

Strengthening

Straws can be joined together for added strength

Use sticky tape or elastic bands

Making a **corner joint.....................**

✤ What can you make, using these methods of joining Artstraws? Here are some ideas to try.

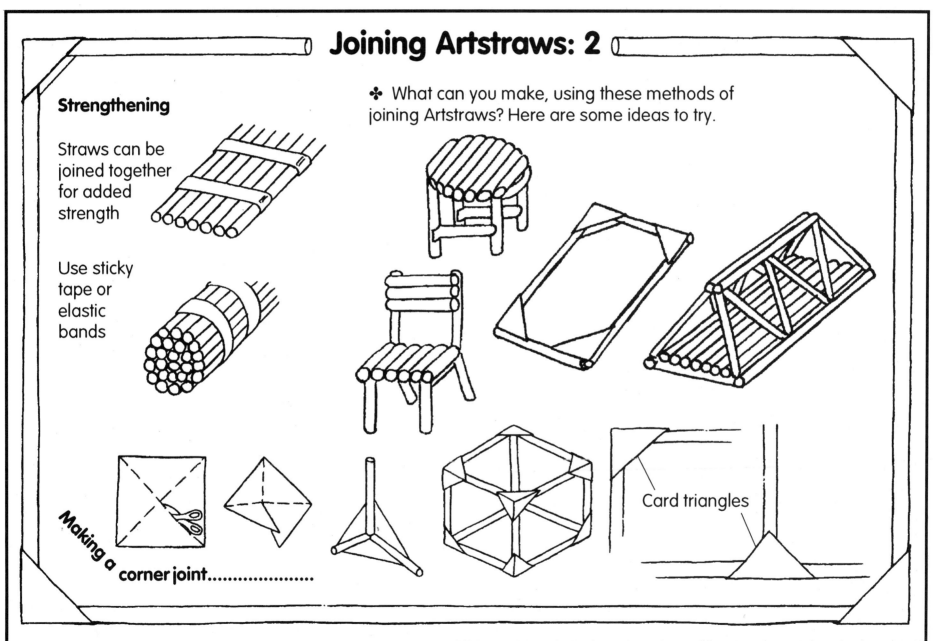

Card triangles

Name _____

Joining Artstraws: 3

❖ Try out some of these ways of making moving joints.

Rotating joint
Different sizes of straw can be made to slide or rotate with each other

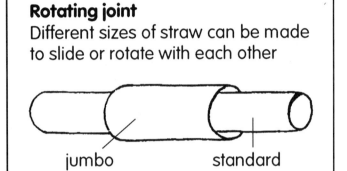

jumbo   standard

Wheels
Wheels can be made by rolling flattened straws around a pencil

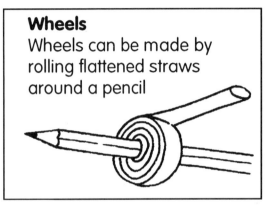

Hinged joint

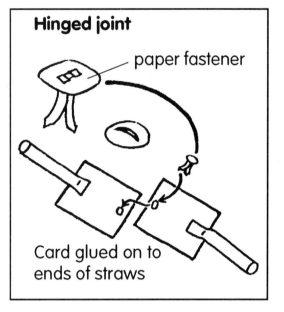

paper fastener

Card glued on to ends of straws

❖ Think of some ways to use these joints. Here are some ideas:

Gate   Axles   See-saw   Swing

Joining Artstraws: 4

Tudor houses were made from wattle and daub panels.

✤ Cut wood to the size of this rectangle.

✤ Make a rectangle from square section wood joined with card triangle corners.

✤ Weave some flattened Artstraws to fit the rectangle as shown below.

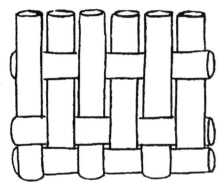

✤ Glue it into place and cover it with papier mâché pulp or plaster mix. Allow it to dry thoroughly.

✤ Join your rectangles together to make a model of a Tudor house.

Name _____

Artstraws

Skinny Stan the Artstraw man

✤ Cut out these templates for Stan's head, hands and feet.

✤ Copy or stick them on to card for added strength.

✤ Now use pieces of Artstraw, string and glue to make Skinny Stan's body, arms and legs.

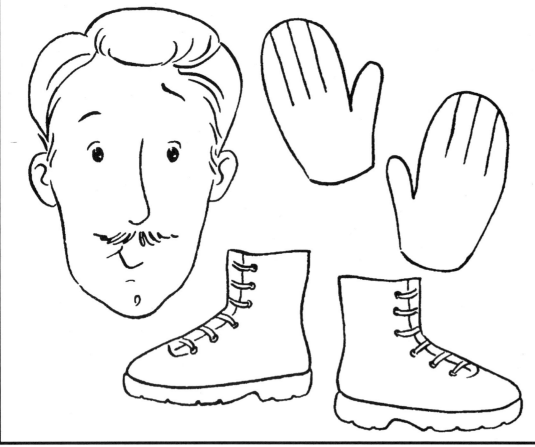

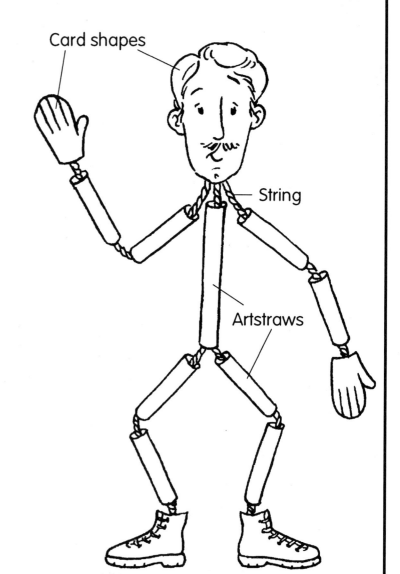

Card shapes

String

Artstraws

Name _____

Home Sweet Home

♣ Cut wood to fit and glue it around the frame of the house.

Copy or stick this frame on to thin card.

Timber

Viking house: 1

✤ Why not make a Viking house? First, make the base by sticking or copying this shape on to card, then cutting it out.

✤ Cut out two wooden strips for the sides and two for the ends. Glue them in place.

✤ Score and fold the roof supports.

✤ Move on to page 31.

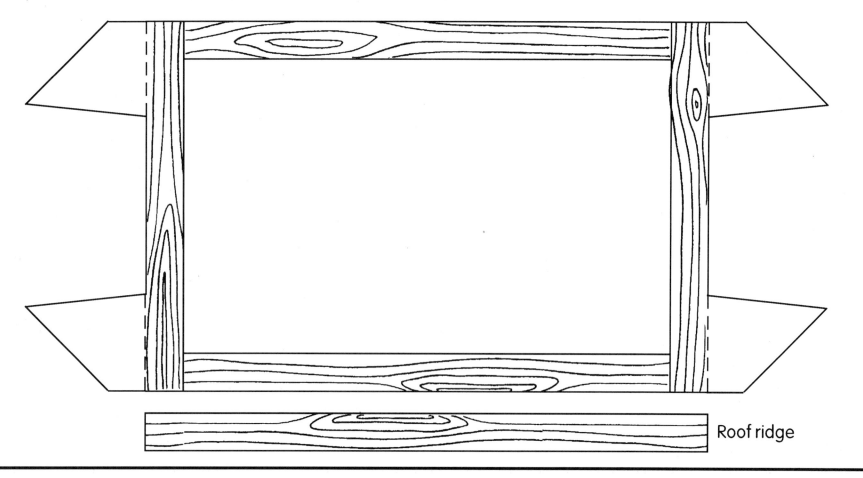

Roof ridge

Viking House: 2

✤ Cut four wooden roof sides and joiners using the template below.

✤ Next make a roof ridge and glue it on to the two card roof joiners.

✤ Finally, glue the roof sides into position and join these to the base.

How will you cover the frame for your house?

Roof joiners

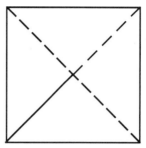 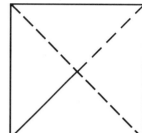

Roof side × 4

Timber

Techniques for joining wood

♣ Experiment with the following ways of joining wood.

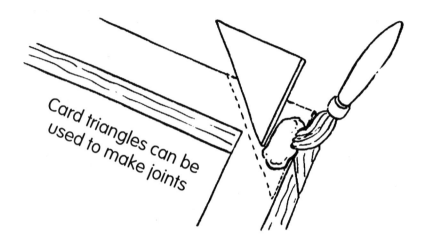

Card triangles can be used to make joints

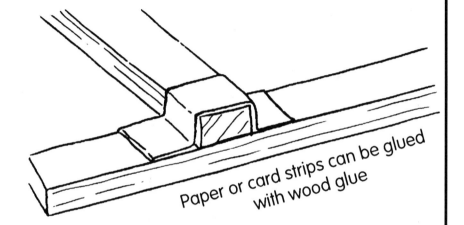

Paper or card strips can be glued with wood glue

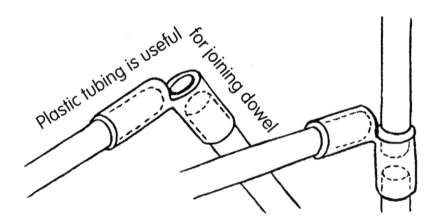

Plastic tubing is useful for joining dowel

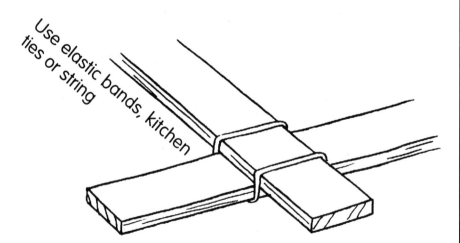

Use elastic bands, kitchen ties or string

2D corner joints

——— cut

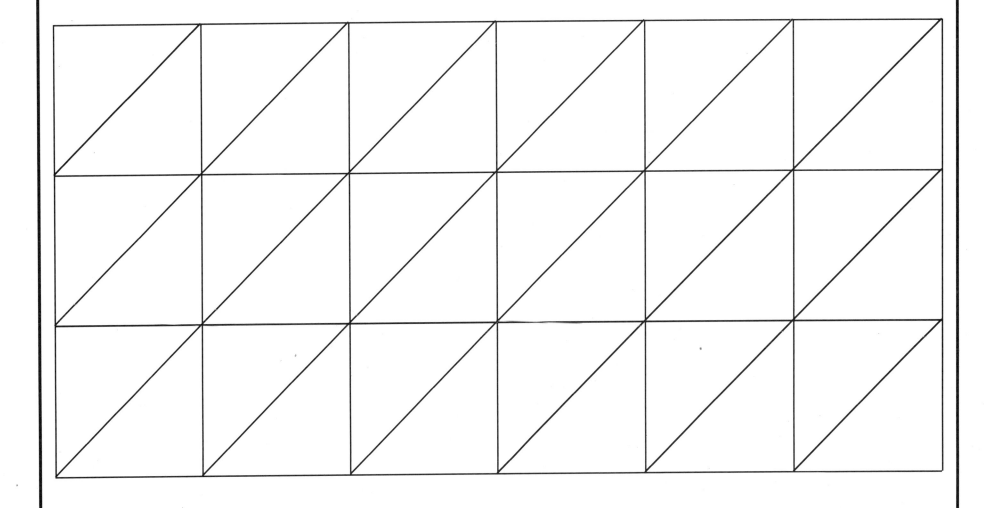

Name _____

Timber

3D corner joints

——— cut

----- score

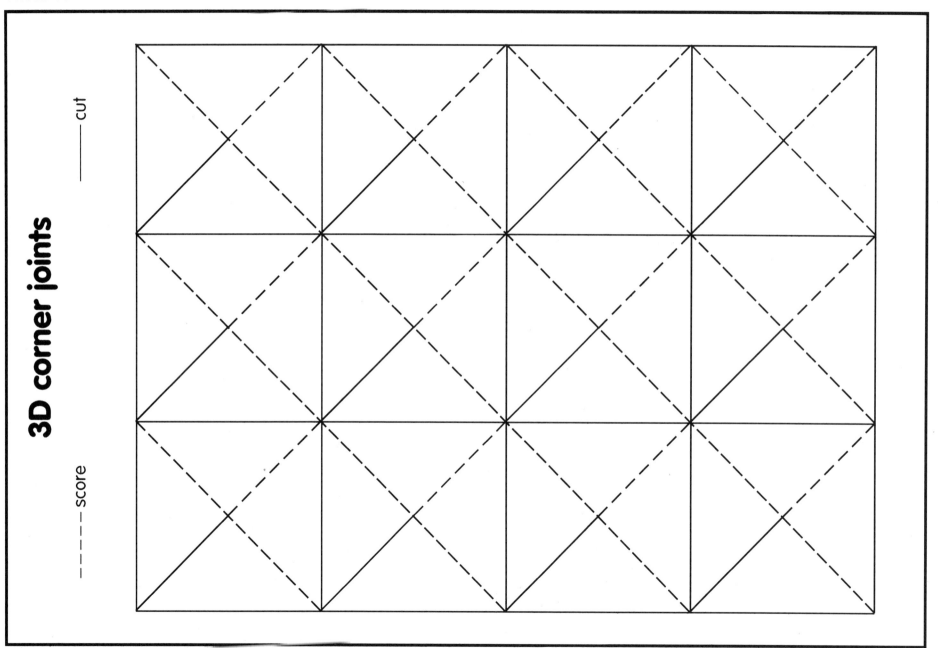

Safety and hygiene

✤ Make a list of all the things you must remember to do before you work with food. Once you have finished your list, check against this page to see how many points you remembered.

Tie your hair back so that it will not dangle into food.

Wash your hands before you start and cover any cuts with a plaster.

Make sure your work surface is clean.

Wipe up any spills quickly.

Take your jumper off and roll up long sleeves.

Wear a clean overall or apron. It's easy to make one with a tea-towel and tape, or wear an old shirt with the cuffs cut off.

Don't lick spoons or fingers!

Food

Fresh fruit salad

What you need:
Any fresh fruit (apples, pears, grapes, kiwi, plums, melons, cherries, nectarines, bananas or strawberries);
200ml fresh fruit juice;
one tablespoon lemon juice (this stops the fruit from going brown).

What to do:
Wash the fruit, and peel, if you wish.
Cut it into small pieces, being careful to remove stalks, pips and stones.

Put the chopped fruit into a bowl and gently mix together with the fruit juice and lemon juice.
Sprinkle a little sugar over it if you wish to make it sweeter.
Put the bowl of fruit salad in the fridge to chill for an hour or more.

✣ Think about the colours of the fruits you choose.
How will you serve it to make it look appealing?

Tropical taster

My drink is called _____

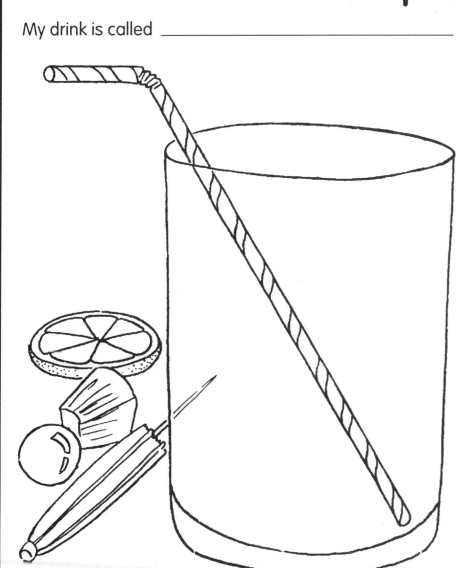

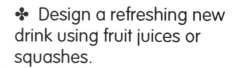

♣ Design a refreshing new drink using fruit juices or squashes.

♣ Add lemonade, mineral water or spring water and slices of fresh fruit if you wish.

♣ Decorate the drink with flags, umbrellas or straws – you could even try frosting the top of the glass with sugar or salt.

♣ Think carefully about how your drink could be presented, then draw it in this empty glass, using labels to show the ingredients you used.

♣ Finally, think of a name for your new drink.

Name _____

Food

Iced biscuits

What you need:
250g plain flour
125g margarine
125g sugar
1 small egg (beaten)
125g icing sugar
1–2 tablespoons water
Baking trays
Large mixing bowl
Small bowl
Wooden spoon
Sieve
Rolling pin
Assorted cutters
Spoons
Knife
Cooling rack
Oven setting:
190°C (375°F),
or Gas Mark 5

What to do:
Grease two baking trays.
Beat the margarine and sugar together in a large bowl until light and fluffy.
Beat in the egg a little at a time.
Sift in the flour. Mix well to make a firm dough.
Sprinkle your work surface and rolling pin with flour (so the dough doesn't stick!), then roll out the dough until it is about 0.5cm thick. Cut out shapes of your choice. Then gather up any scraps of dough and repeat until it is all used up. Put the biscuits on the trays.
Bake them in the oven for about 15 minutes until light brown.
Put the biscuits on a wire rack to cool.

When the biscuits are cool, mix the icing sugar and water together in a bowl until smooth. Spread icing evenly on to each biscuit.
• What colour will your icing be (add a few drops of food colouring)?
• How does your icing taste (try adding flavourings)?

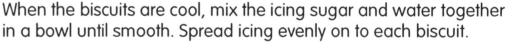

Fancy sandwiches

Hold a sandwich-making competition to see who can come up with the best new sandwich.

♣ Think about:

Bread
Bread or rolls, crispbreads or crackers? Brown, white or granary? Will it be an open or closed sandwich?

Fillings
Crunchy or smooth? Moist or dry? Sweet or savoury? Look at this table for ideas.

Shape
How will you cut the bread – triangles, circles, rectangles – or other shapes, using biscuit cutters?

Garnish
Will you use any garnish – perhaps cress or parsley?

Display
How will you present your sandwich – on a plate or a bowl, with a napkin or labels?

Name _____

Pizza

❖ Organise a pizza party.

What you need:
Base: 100g white or wholemeal flour, 50g block margarine, milk, 50g grated cheddar cheese.
Topping: 1 small tin of tomatoes, 1 small chopped onion, 50g grated cheddar cheese, salt, pepper and herbs.
Oven setting: 220°C or Gas Mark 7.

What to do:
Lightly grease a baking sheet.
Rub the margarine into the flour until it resembles breadcrumbs, then mix in the cheese.
Stir in the milk until the dough sticks together, then roll it out into a circle.
Mix the tomato and onion together and spread this topping over the pizza base. Add other toppings of your choice.
Sprinkle the cheese and herbs on top.
Ask an adult to place it in the oven for about 15 minutes.
What is your favourite topping? Try sliced sausage, bacon, ham, sliced mushrooms, tuna, sweetcorn, peppers, pineapple.

❖ Draw and label your pizza on the back of this sheet. Choose a name for it.

Button it!

♣ Copy or stick this page on to thin card.

♣ Sew a button in the centre of each flower. Use buttons and threads with bright colours to attract the bees!

♣ Colour in the flowers.

♣ Finish off by covering the vase with sticky paper.

Textiles

Teddy's bed

Poor old teddy is tired. He needs a bed to sleep in.

❖ Cut out a rectangle of card (20 × 30cm) and mark it as shown on the diagram below.

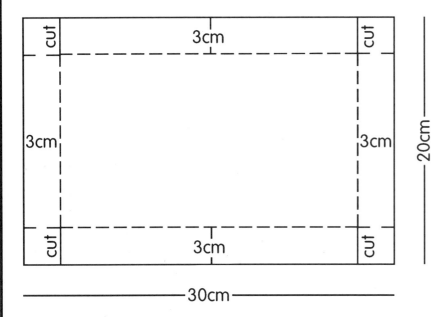

❖ Pop teddy inside or lie him on top.

❖ Design and make a headboard for teddy's bed.

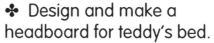

❖ Glue your card template on to fabric.

❖ Cut and score, then glue the flaps to make a bed.

Ready for bed

Why not make a pillow and quilt for teddy's bed (page 42)?

What you need:
Cotton or polyester fabric
Stuffing
Needle and thread
Material for trimming

✤ Choose some suitable fabric, then cut out two rectangular shapes 18 × 22cm for the quilt and two rectangular shapes 7 × 10cm for the pillow.

✤ Now choose some trimming (lace perhaps or braid).

✤ Cut one piece 18cm long and one piece 7cm long.

✤ Pin and stitch the trimming in place on the right side of one piece of pillow material and one piece of quilt.

✤ With the wrong sides together, sew your pillow and quilt pieces together using running stitch or back stitch 1cm from the edge.

✤ Turn inside out and fill with stuffing.

✤ Pin the open edges together, then oversew to join them along the edge.

Textiles

❖ From this pattern cut out a piece of light polyester or cotton.

❖ Stitch a length of lace in place at the top on the right side.

❖ Fold in half along the fold line so that the lace is on the inside.

❖ Join the bag at the side and bottom using small running stitch or backstitch.

❖ Turn the bag inside out and fill it with pot-pourri or lavender.

❖ Tie up the neck of the bag with a length of ribbon, finishing with a bow.

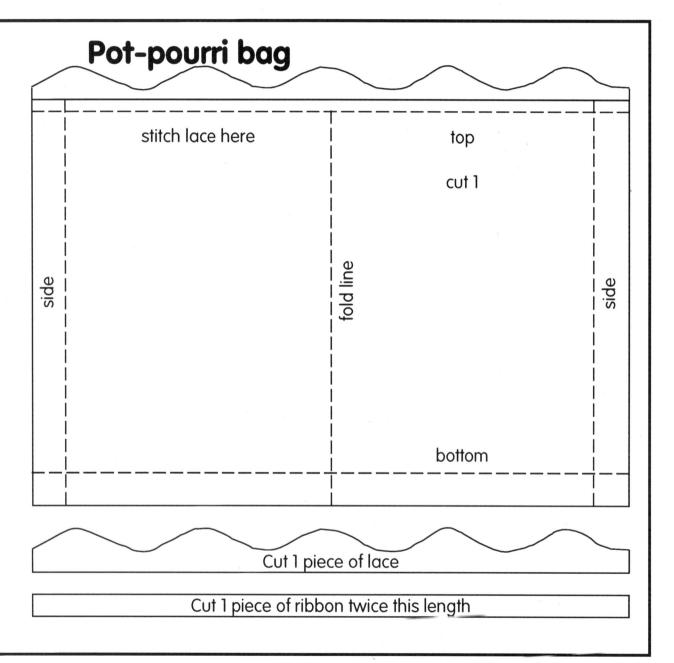

Pot-pourri bag

stitch lace here

top

cut 1

side

fold line

side

bottom

Cut 1 piece of lace

Cut 1 piece of ribbon twice this length

44

Name _____

Sam the scarecrow

It's windy, and all Sam's clothes
have blown away! Can you
make some scarecrow clothes?

✦ Stick two lollipop sticks
to this outline.

♣ Cut out fabric scraps
and glue them on – will
you give Sam trousers or
a skirt? What about a
warm hat or cosy scarf?

♣ Use straw or wool for
hands and feet.

Name _____

Textiles

Fred bear

- ✤ Cut out Fred bear in card.

- ✤ Punch holes in the places marked.

- ✤ Take a long piece of coloured ribbon, wool or string. Give it a collar of masking tape or thread it through a bodkin or blunt needle.

- ✤ Fasten the loose end in place on the wrong side with tape.

- ✤ Sew in and out of the holes, finishing off on the wrong side and sticking the loose end down with tape.

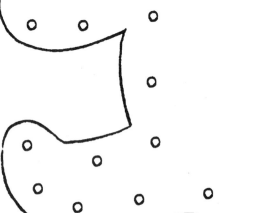

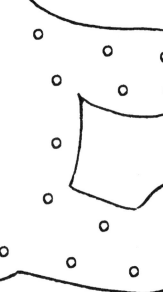

Clara the caterpillar

✤ Cut out five pieces of felt for Clara's body and face.
Stick these into place, starting at Clara's bottom!

✤ Cut out eight pieces of felt for Clara's legs. Stick these into place.

✤ Use scraps of felt for her eyes, nose and mouth. Stick these on.

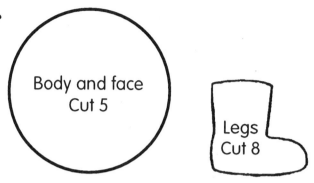

Body and face
Cut 5

Legs
Cut 8

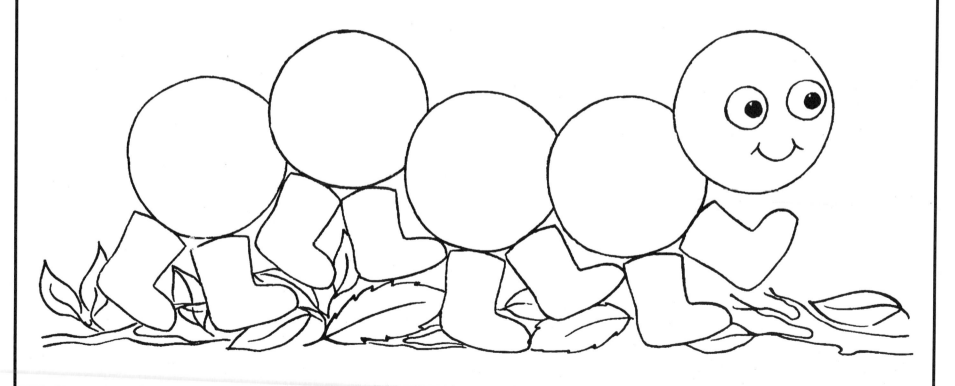

Construction kits

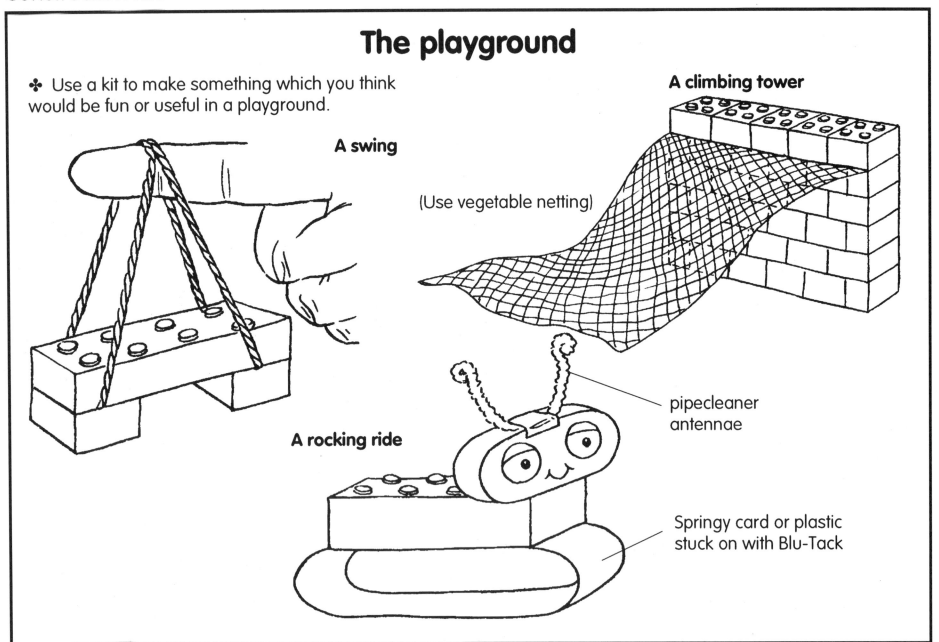

The playground

❖ Use a kit to make something which you think would be fun or useful in a playground.

A swing

A climbing tower

(Use vegetable netting)

A rocking ride

pipecleaner antennae

Springy card or plastic stuck on with Blu-Tack

Name _____

The fairground

❖ Use a kit to make a thrilling ride for a fairground.

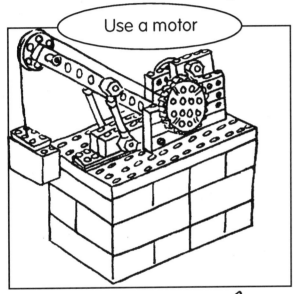

Use a motor

Masking tape

Join kits together

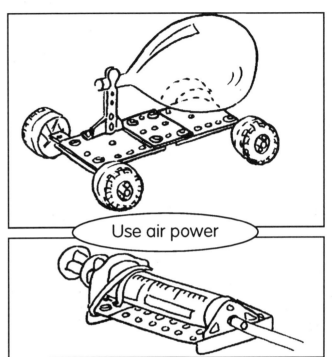

Use air power

Motorise your model with a kit mechanism

Tape or hot glue

Sleeve of valve tubing

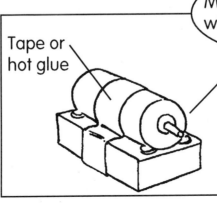

Malleable materials

Working with dough

Try working with dough-like materials such as play dough, Plasticine or clay.

❖ Make solid shapes such as cylinders, cones, cuboids, triangular prisms and prisms, then join these shapes together to make objects.

❖ Roll it out using a rolling pin, a plastic bottle full of water or a piece of thick dowel.

❖ Make rolls and join these together to make hollow 3D shapes.

❖ Plait them or twist them together.

❖ Use cutters to cut out shapes.

❖ Make impressions and patterns.

Use some of these ideas to make a piece of jewellery or an ornamental pot.

Barney the bull

Farmer Brown needs a new fence to keep Barney the bull in his field.

♣ Can you build a fence for him?
Use one of the following ideas for your frame.

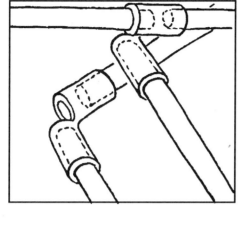

Plastic tubing is useful for joining dowel

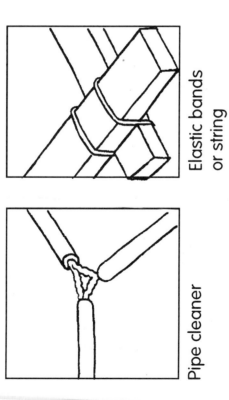

Elastic bands or string

Pipe cleaner

Construction kit parts

Use nuts and bolts

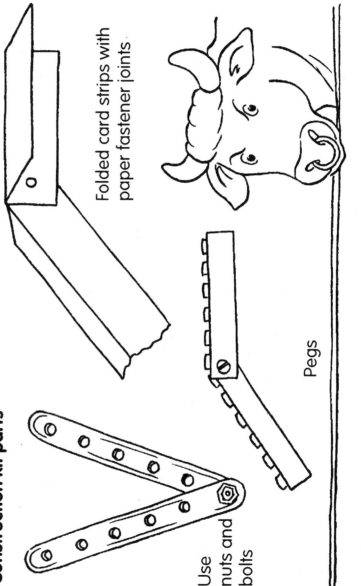

Folded card strips with paper fastener joints

Pegs

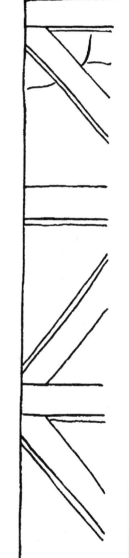

Name _____

Structures

Frame it!

♣ Look at the ideas on page 51, then make some of these shapes from pipe cleaners, tubes, wood, paper, card or construction kits. Which ones are rigid (difficult to push over)?

♣ Name each shape.

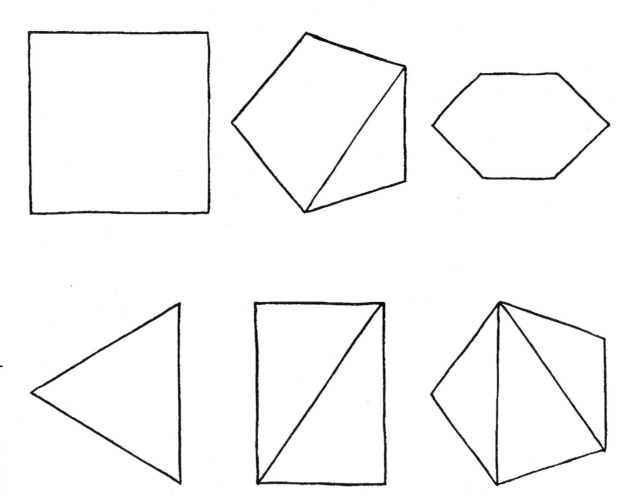

♣ If it is not rigid, draw lines to show how you could make it rigid. Which shape is needed to make each of these frames rigid?

♣ Use what you have found out to make a strong frame for a tent. How will you cover it?

Teacher Timesavers: Technology

Name _____

Strong beams

♣ Use sheets of scrap paper or thin card to try out these ideas for strength. Use adhesive, Blu-Tack or tape to hold them together.

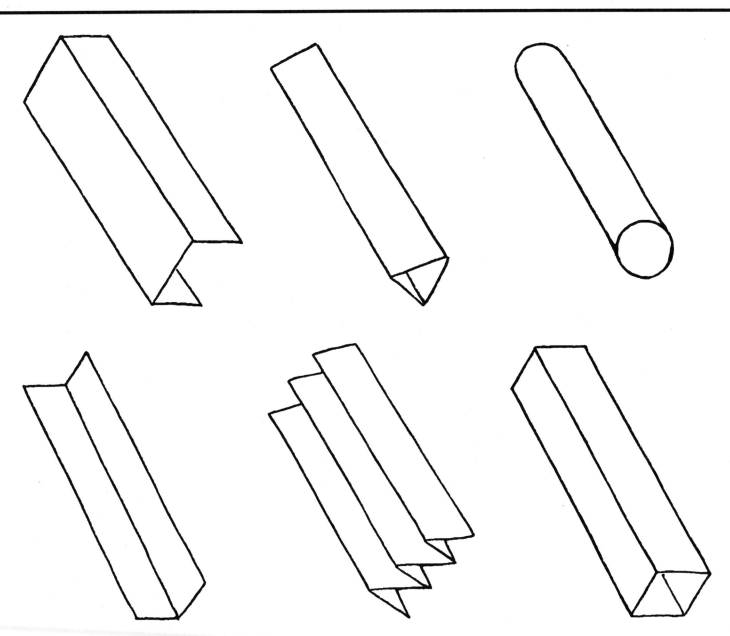

Which shape makes the strongest beam?
How can you set up a fair test to find out?

Name _____

Structures

Stability

✤ Make some of these tower structures from Artstraws.

Try using: bigger bases

heavier bases – possibly weighted with Plasticine or Blu-Tack.

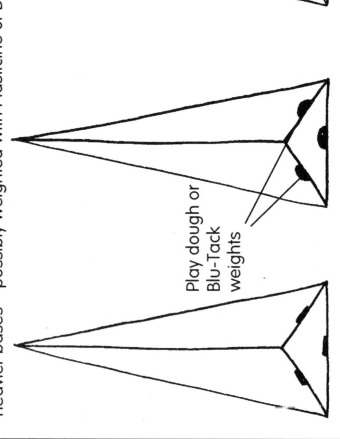

Play dough or Blu-Tack weights

Which towers are more difficult to push over?

How can you set up a fair test to find out?

Investigating cardboard boxes

✤ Find the seams where an old cardboard box is joined together.

✤ Carefully slide a finger or a ruler down the seams to open them out.

✤ Lay the card out flat to see how the box has been made. This is called a **net**.

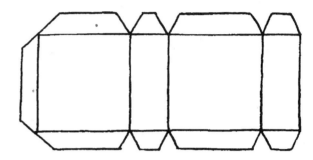

✤ Copy the net on to card or squared paper. Can you make your own box by cutting this out, scoring, folding and sticking it down?

✤ Use your box to make a moving vehicle.

Name _____

Corrugated card or plastics

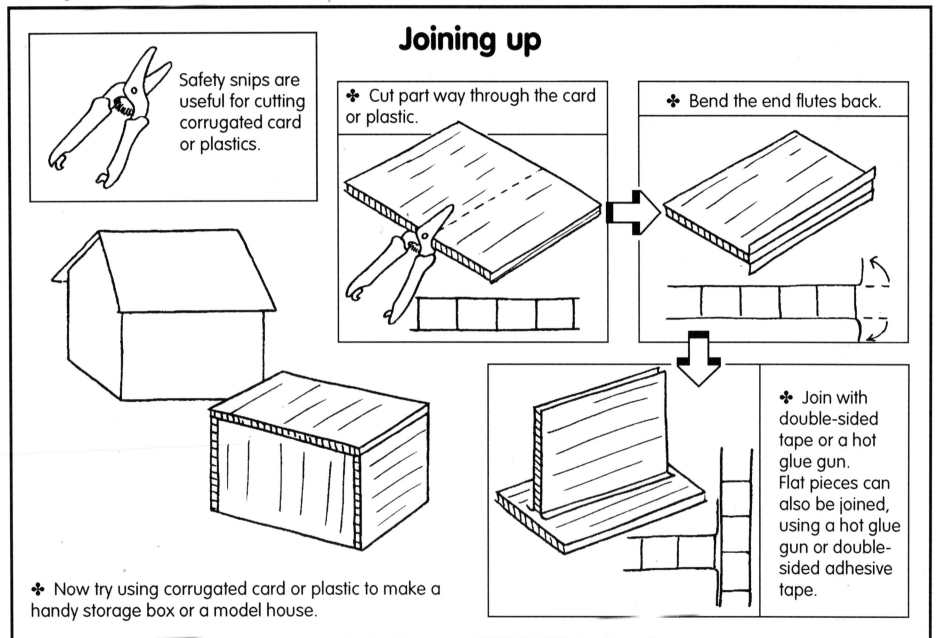

Joining up

Safety snips are useful for cutting corrugated card or plastics.

✤ Cut part way through the card or plastic.

✤ Bend the end flutes back.

✤ Join with double-sided tape or a hot glue gun. Flat pieces can also be joined, using a hot glue gun or double-sided adhesive tape.

✤ Now try using corrugated card or plastic to make a handy storage box or a model house.

Matching the names

♣ Join each tool to its name by drawing lines.

♣ Can you describe how each tool works?

scissors

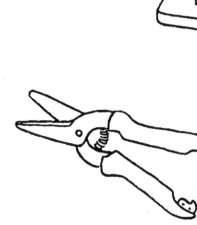

double hole punch

junior hacksaw

single hole punch

safety snips

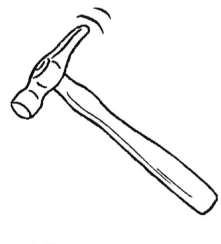

hand drill

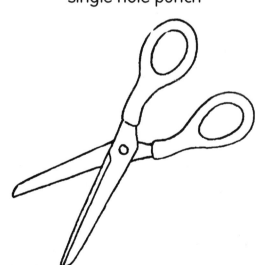

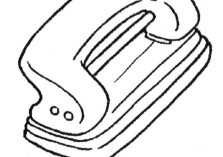

hammer

Vocabulary

Name _____

Using simple hand tools

♣ Draw and label some hand tools you have used.
The first one has been drawn for you.

This is a

It is used to

This is a

It is used to

This is a

It is used to

This is a

It is used to

Simple hand tools: wood

♣ Label these tools from the list of names down the side of the page.
They are all used for working with wood.

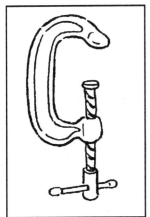	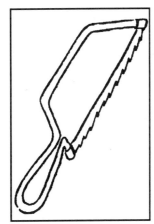	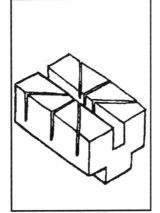	 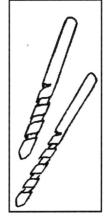
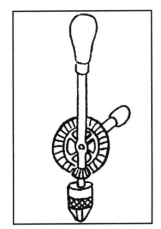	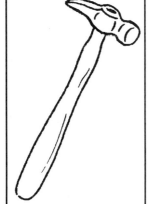	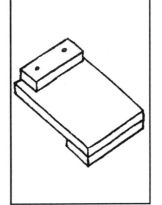	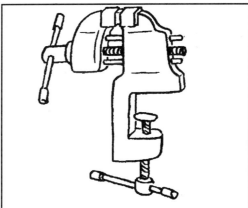

hammer

junior hacksaw

timber joining jig

hand drill

sawing jig

'G' clamp

bench hook

drill bits

portable table vice

♣ Colour in any of the tools that you have used.

Vocabulary

Name _____

Simple hand tools: fabric

All these tools are used with fabric.

✣ Can you find out what they are called and label them?

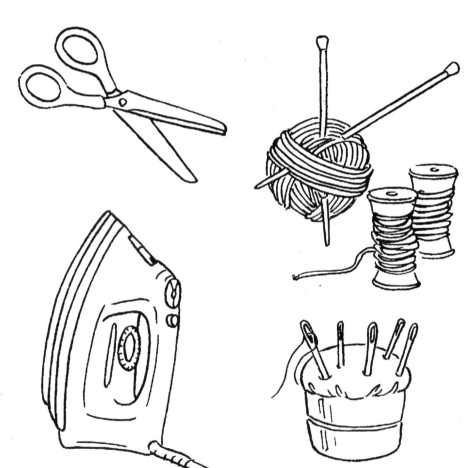

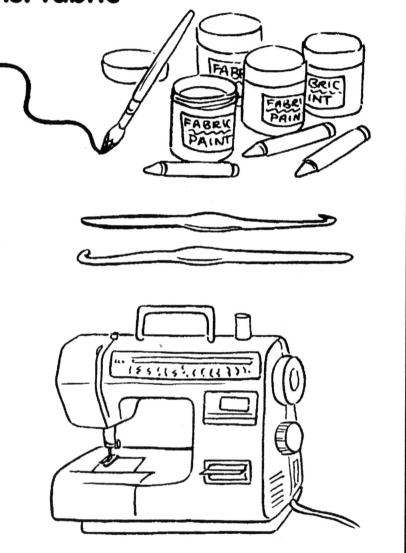

Simple hand tools: food

✤ Complete this sheet in the school kitchen or at home.

✤ Find out the name of each piece of equipment shown here.

✤ On the back of this sheet, explain how each tool is used.

Name _____

Assessment

Greetings cards

Is there anyone you would like to send a special card to?

❖ Design and make a card which has at least one moving part.
The moving part could be hinged, sliding, spinning or pop up.

Here are some ideas you may like to use.

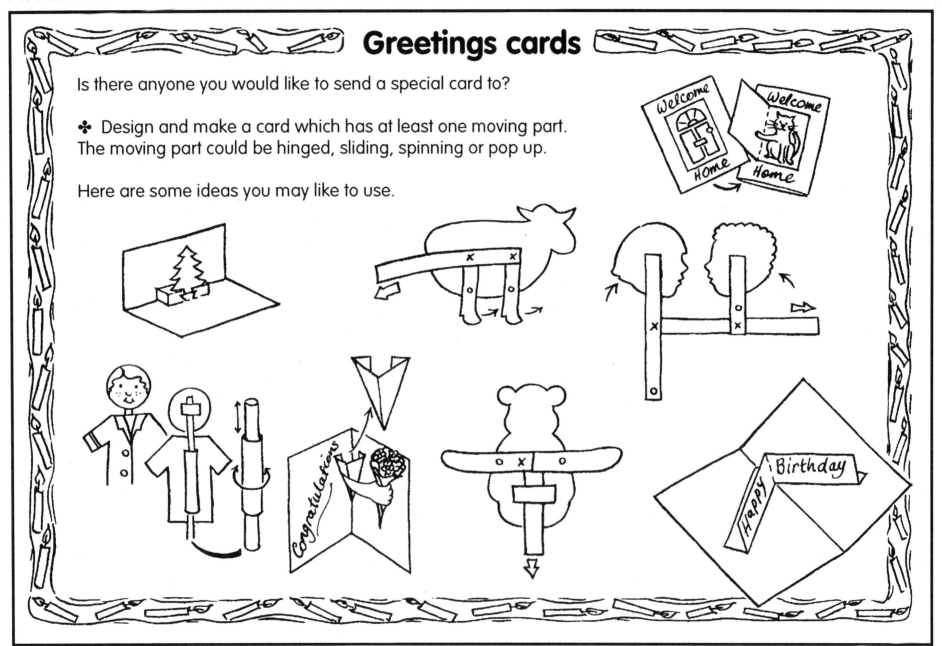

Dick Whittington

Dick Whittington went to London, later he became Lord Mayor.

Most buildings at that time were made with timber frames like the ones shown here.

♣ Can you make a house for Dick Whittington to live in with his family?

Don't forget to leave room for his cat!

Name _____

Assessment

Island life

Robinson Crusoe needs to make his life on the island more comfortable.
He has a good supply of timber, card, glue, string and fabrics from the shipwreck.

✤ Design some simple items of furniture for Robinson Crusoe.

✤ Record your ideas below and on the other side of the sheet. You will need headings like those listed here.

• What I think Robinson Crusoe needs most

• My original designs

• The materials I will use are

• The tools I will use are

• This is what I did

✤ At the end, record any changes that you made to your original designs.

Name _____

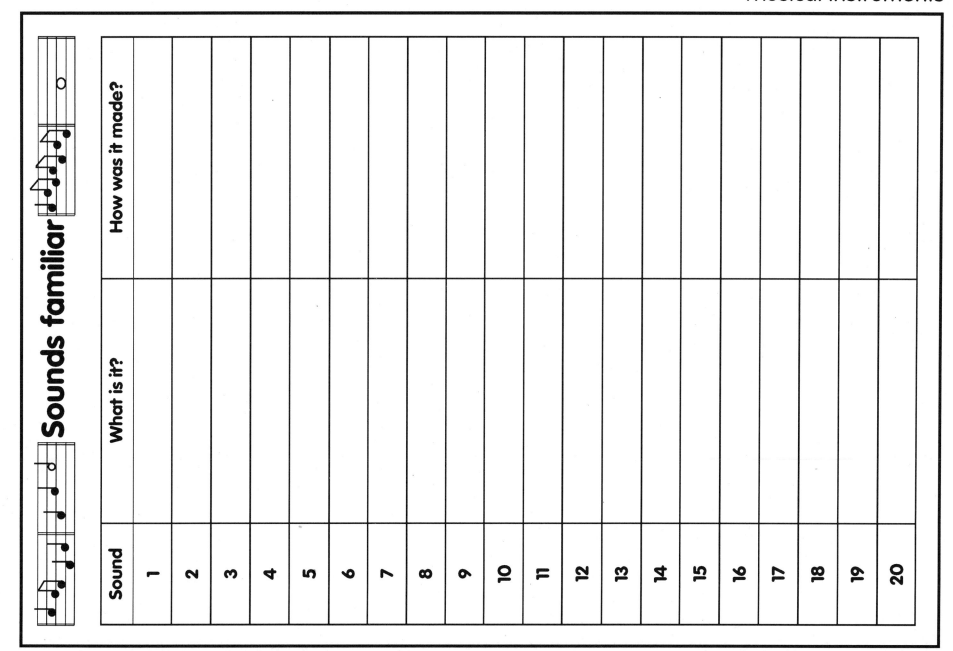

Sounds familiar

Sound	What is it?	How was it made?
1		
2		
3		
4		
5		
6		
7		
8		
9		
10		
11		
12		
13		
14		
15		
16		
17		
18		
19		
20		

Name _____

Musical instruments

Blow it!

Can you make a musical instrument from Artstraws?

You will need:
Artstraws (both jumbo and standard), dowel and scissors.

✤ Draw and describe your instrument here.

✤ Join straws of different lengths to make pan pipes.

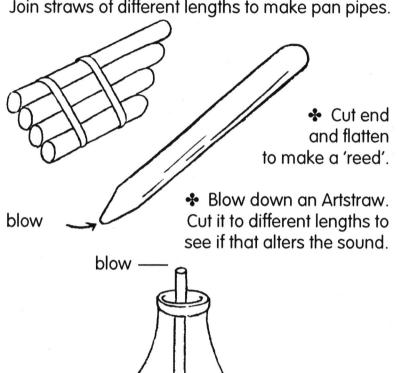

blow

✤ Cut end and flatten to make a 'reed'.

✤ Blow down an Artstraw. Cut it to different lengths to see if that alters the sound.

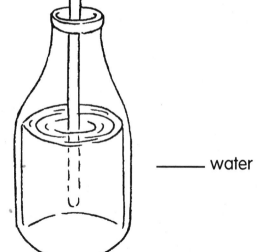

blow ———

——— water

If your Artstraws won't make a sound try one of these ideas:

Name _____

Shake it all about!

✤ Make some shakers from washing-up liquid bottles.

✤ Use various fillings.

● Can you guess what is inside the bottles just by shaking them?

● Does it make any difference to the sound if you shake them in different ways?

● What happens if you use other fillings?

● What happens if you put the filling into different containers?

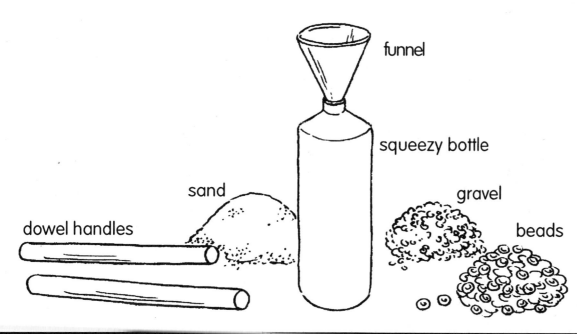

Join in with the band!

♣ Can you make a sound using an elastic band?

● What happens to the sound if you use a thicker band?

● What happens if you make the band tighter?

● What happens to the band while it is making a sound?

● Can you make the sound any louder?

♣ Make a simple plucked instrument.
Copy the one shown below, or design your own.

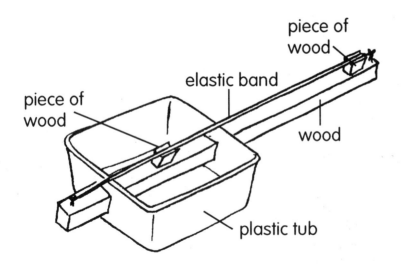

piece of wood

elastic band

piece of wood

wood

plastic tub

Get with the beat

✤ Try tapping a range of different-shaped containers.

• How does the sound change?

• Does it make any difference what you use to tap them with?

• Does it make any difference how they are tapped?

• Does it make any difference what the container is made of?

✤ Try making an unusual musical instrument which can be tapped.

• Think of a good name for it.

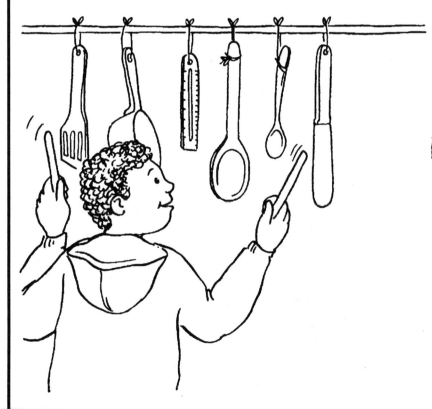

coconut halves or yoghurt pots

balloon

elastic band

tin can drum

beaters

Musical instruments

Name _____

Getting into a scrape

♣ Try using a dowel scraper to scrape objects with different textures.

• What different sounds can you make by scraping?

• Does it make a difference how you hold the scraper?

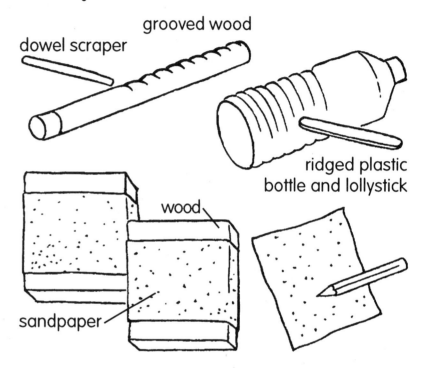

dowel scraper   grooved wood

ridged plastic bottle and lollystick

wood

sandpaper

• What differences do you notice when you scrape different surfaces?

• Does it make a difference if you use different scrapers?

♣ Use some of the ideas shown on this page to make your own scraper.

Good vibrations!

❧ Make a sound by twanging a ruler on the edge of a desk.

• Does it make any difference if you use a wooden or a plastic ruler?

• How can you change the sound?

• Does the sound change if you use longer or shorter lengths of ruler?

• Does it make a difference if you twang them on different objects?

❧ Now try making sounds using a comb and paper.

• What do you have to do to make a sound?

• What can you feel?

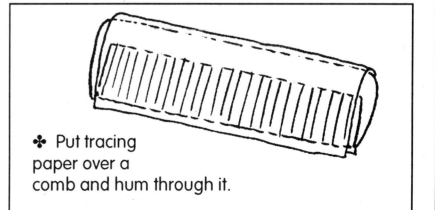

❧ Put tracing paper over a comb and hum through it.

Name _____

Paper engineering

Windmill net: 1

♣ Trace or copy this shape on to card.

♣ Colour it in, then cut it out carefully.

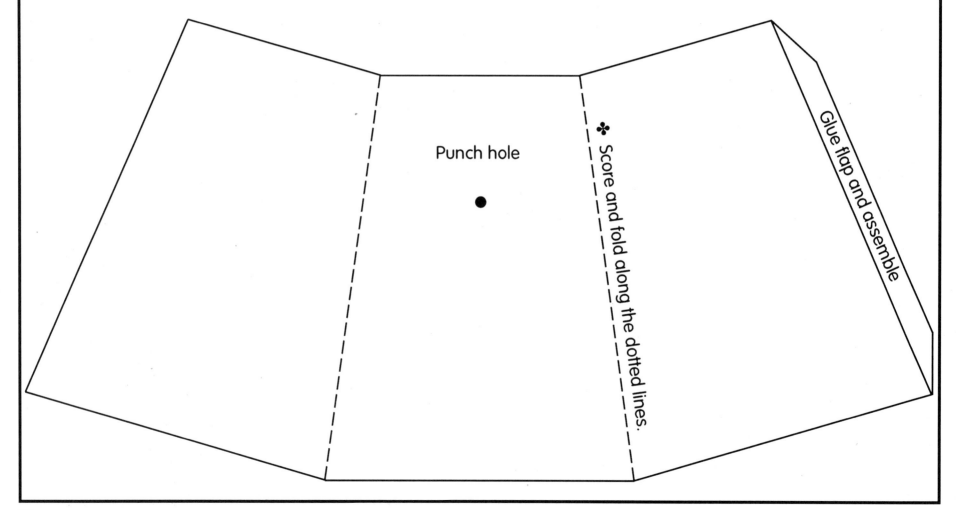

Punch hole

♣ Score and fold along the dotted lines.

Glue flap and assemble

Name _____

Windmill net: 2

♣ Copy or trace both shapes on to card before you begin.

♣ Cut out the sail and punch a hole in the centre.

♣ Join the sail to the windmill building with a paper fastener **before** you complete it by sticking down the final flap.

♣ Cut out the roof shape along the solid lines. Score and fold along the dotted lines.

♣ Fold one side of the roof over and stick it down.

♣ Set the roof on the building (page 72), or glue it in place.

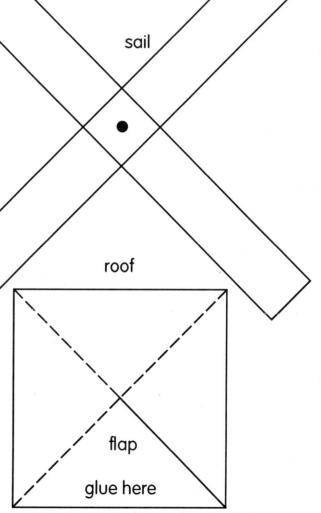

sail

roof

flap

glue here

Paper engineering

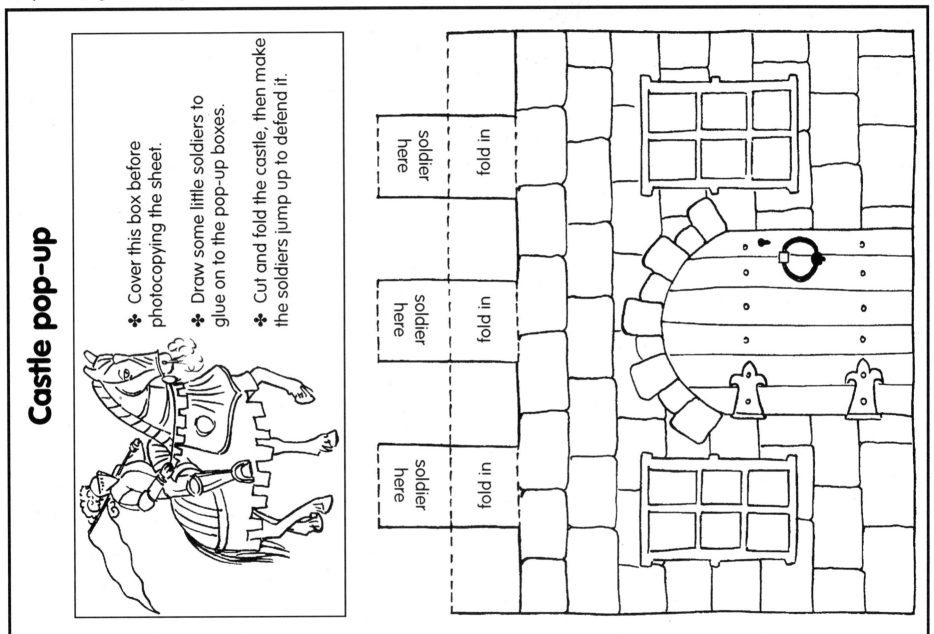

Castle pop-up

❖ Cover this box before photocopying the sheet.

❖ Draw some little soldiers to glue on to the pop-up boxes.

❖ Cut and fold the castle, then make the soldiers jump up to defend it.

soldier here — fold in

soldier here — fold in

soldier here — fold in

Name _____

Haunted castle

✤ Copy or glue this sheet on to card.

✤ Cut the windows and door, scoring and folding the hinge side so that they will all open.

✤ Draw some ghostly ghouls and monstrous surprises to glue behind them.

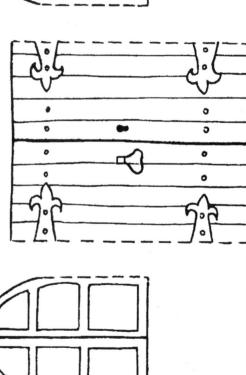

Name _____

It's magic

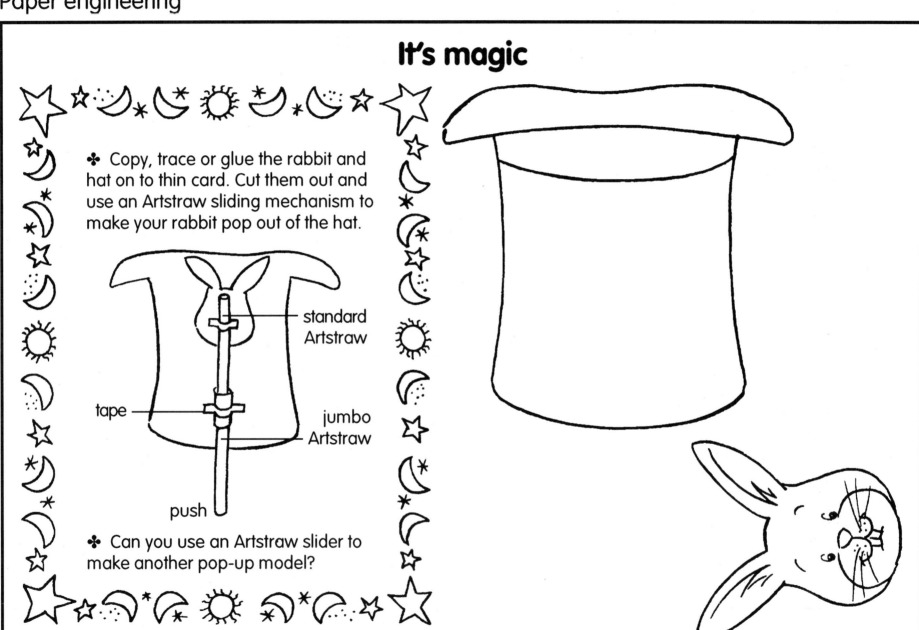

♣ Copy, trace or glue the rabbit and hat on to thin card. Cut them out and use an Artstraw sliding mechanism to make your rabbit pop out of the hat.

standard Artstraw

tape

jumbo Artstraw

push

♣ Can you use an Artstraw slider to make another pop-up model?

Time on your hands

✣ Copy or glue the clock face on to thin card.

✣ Cut out the two hands and punch holes.

✣ Fix the two hands on to the clock face with a paper fastener joint.

✣ Colour and decorate the clock in any way you choose.

✣ Use your clock to practise telling the time.

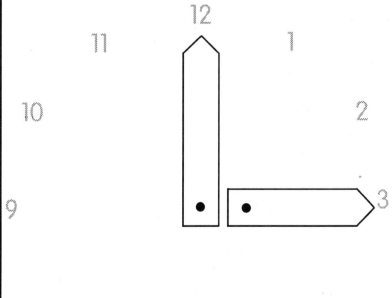

Paper engineering

Life goes sliding by

♣ Copy or glue this countryside picture on to thin card.

♣ Cut a slit along the dotted line on the road.

♣ Cut out some card figures or vehicles.

♣ Attach them to card strips or lolly sticks, then slide them down the road.

Pop-up

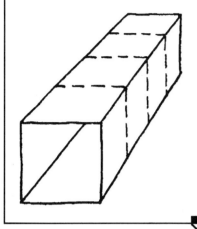

✤ Turn a small cardboard (film) box inside out and glue it together again.

✤ Now flatten it and cut it into strips.

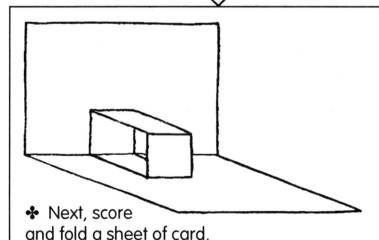

✤ Next, score and fold a sheet of card. Attach the box section inside, with Blu-Tack, so that it will fold flat.

✤ Add various card shapes inside to make a pop-up surprise for someone. Do not use any glue until you are happy that everything fits into place.

Paper engineering

Captain Quack

✤ Cut out the Captain Quack face carefully.

✤ Fold it in half down the central fold line.

✤ Cut and fold the beak so that it can be folded inside.

✤ Glue the finished face inside a fold of card.

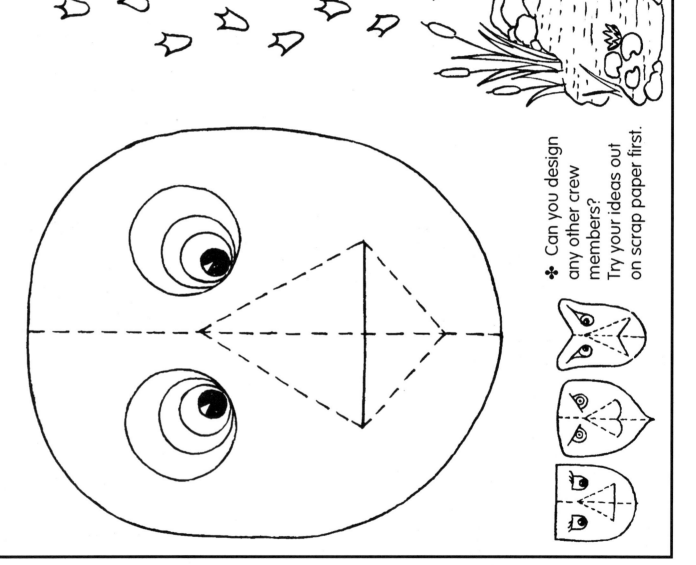

✤ Can you design any other crew members? Try your ideas out on scrap paper first.

Name _____

V-fold surprise

✤ Cut out a shape from card and attach it with Blu-Tack to the V-fold inside the card. Does it pop up when the card is opened and disappear when it is closed?

✤ If not, adjust it until it does, then glue it in place when you are happy with it.

✤ Choose one or two of your favourite people, and use this idea to surprise them with a card!

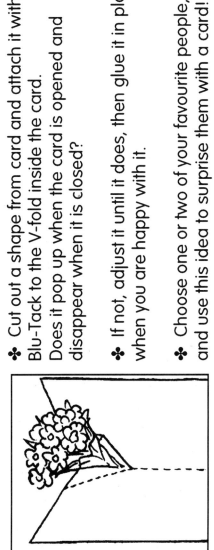

Name _____

Paper engineering

Windy weather: 1

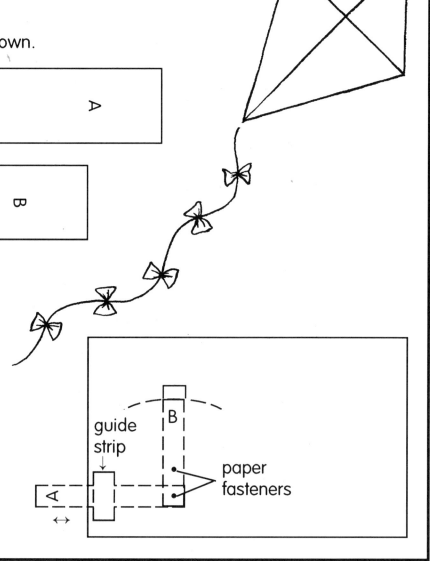

✤ Cut out and join a string and tissue tail to this kite.

✤ Cut out all three strips from card and hole punch where shown.

✤ Cut a slit in the windy weather picture on page 83.

✤ Cut out and fix the kite to the top of strip B, then pull the kite (with its tail) through the slit. Use Blu-Tack first until you are sure everything is in the right place.

✤ Link strips A and B together with a paper fastener. Slide strip A through the slit and join to the picture with a paper fastener. Glue the guide strip in place over strip B.

Windy weather: 2

Wheels and axles

Name _____

Wheely good ideas!

❖ Try some of these ideas for adding wheels to any vehicles you make.

Bead wheels

Dowel axle

Film pot wheels fitted
with a foam insulation tyre

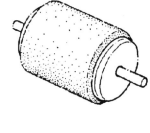

Drink can
'rollers'

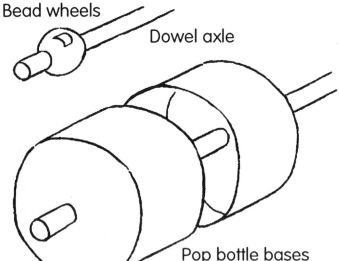

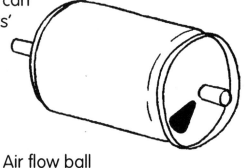

Pop bottle bases

Air flow ball
wheels

Cotton reel wheels

❖ Experiment with these methods of keeping wheels on axles.

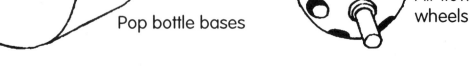

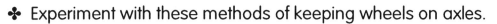

blob of Plasticine,
Blu-Tack or play dough

drawing pin

tubing collar

elastic band

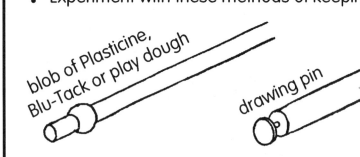

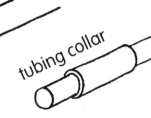

❖ Which kind of wheel do you find the most stable, the fastest, the strongest?

Making a chassis

❖ Try one or two of these ideas for making a chassis (vehicle base).

❖ Then think of a way of turning your chassis into a vehicle.

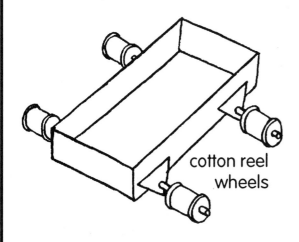

cotton reel wheels

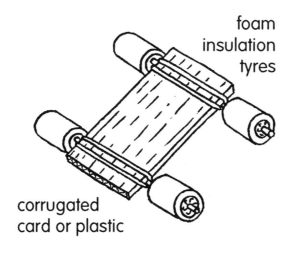

foam insulation tyres

corrugated card or plastic

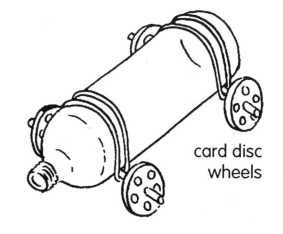

card disc wheels

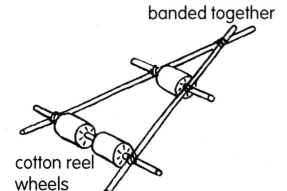

dowel chassis banded together

cotton reel wheels

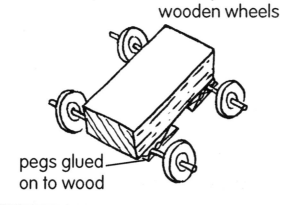

plastic or wooden wheels

pegs glued on to wood

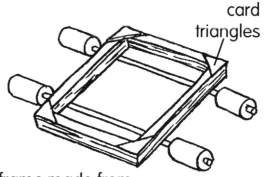

card triangles

frame made from square section wood

Movement in water

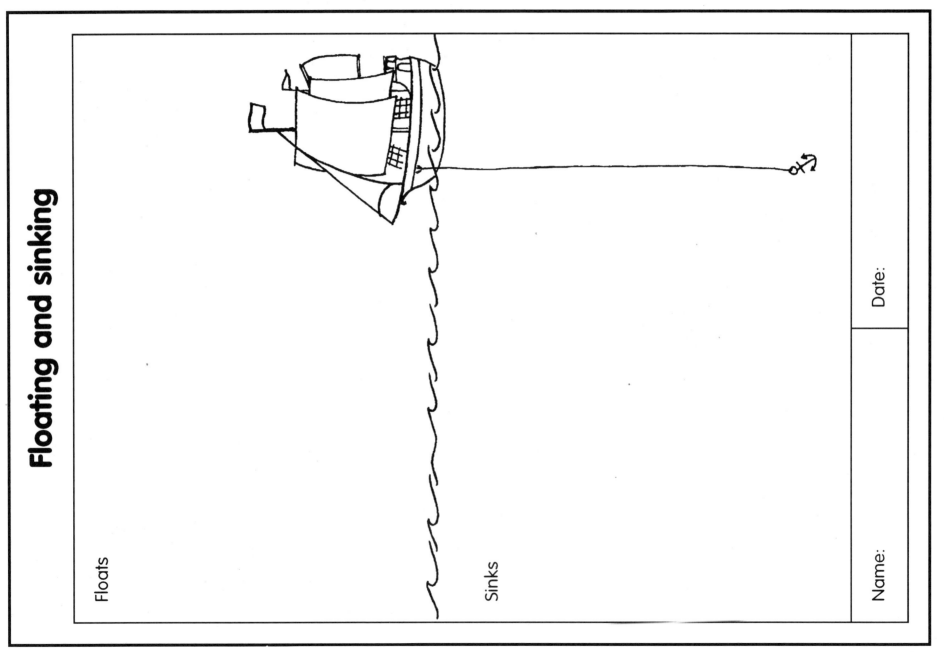

Floating and sinking

Floats

Sinks

Name:

Date:

Name _____

Making boats

♣ Work in groups as design teams.

♣ Build a boat to the design you have been given.

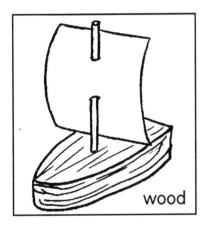

wood

two bottles
banded together
with strips of wood

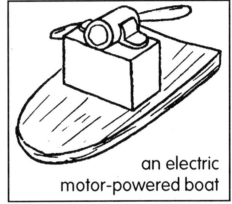

an electric
motor-powered boat

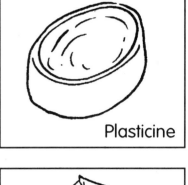

Plasticine

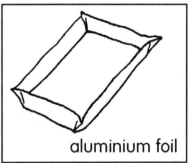

aluminium foil

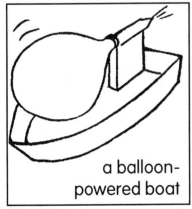

a balloon-
powered boat

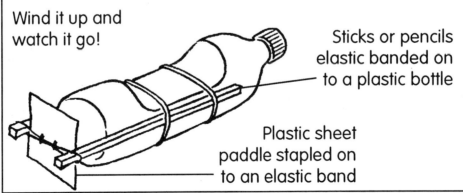

Wind it up and
watch it go!

Sticks or pencils
elastic banded on
to a plastic bottle

Plastic sheet
paddle stapled on
to an elastic band

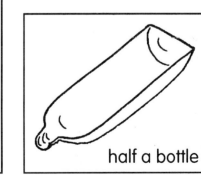

half a bottle

♣ Hold a boat race.   Which design is the best?   Can you say why?

Name _____

Make a spinner

♣ Cut out and fold the spinner.
Does it work?

♣ Can you make it spin in both directions?

♣ Can you make it spin any faster?

♣ Design your own spinner and try it out.

Leonardo da Vinci's parachute

Leonardo da Vinci drew a sketch with a design for a parachute over 500 years ago – in 1485.

♣ Cut out and fold the shape carefully.

♣ Tape a 20cm length of thread to each corner.

♣ Gather the threads together and join them with a Plasticine weight. Does da Vinci's design work? How can you improve it?

♣ Now design your own parachute.

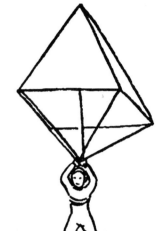

glue flap here

Name _____

Hinges

Hinges

✤ Try some of these ideas for making hinges.

Score card 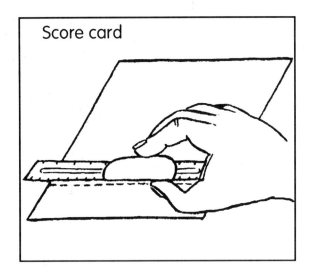	Use tape or fabric glued on 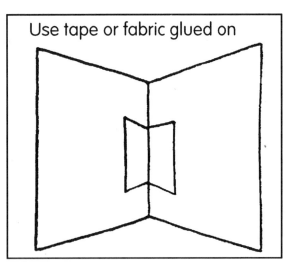	Use string, thread or paper fastener joints 
Use jumbo and standard Artstraws to make a hinge 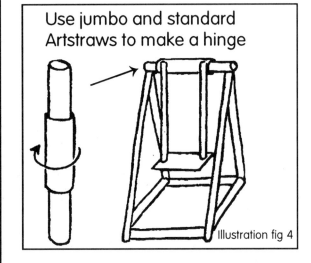 Illustration fig 4	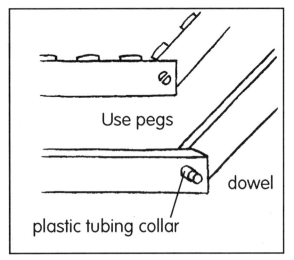 Use pegs plastic tubing collar dowel	lock nut 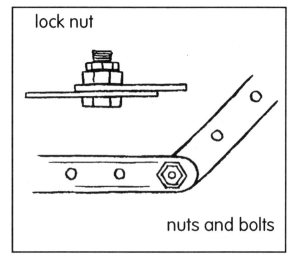 nuts and bolts

Name _____

Introducing levers

Levers have been used throughout history to help move heavy objects.
Levers are used every day to help us perform certain simple tasks.

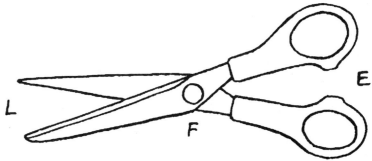

Words about levers

The force used to make a lever work is called the **effort** (E).
The thing to be moved is called the **load** (L) and the point the lever moves around is called the **fulcrum** (F) or the **pivot**.

Investigating levers

✣ Choose something which uses a lever to make it work.

✣ Make a clear labelled sketch of it, then make an exploded diagram showing all its parts separately.

✣ Explain how it works and why it is used.
What do you like about it?
Could it be improved in any way?

Levers

Name _____

Investigating levers

A see-saw is a simple lever system.

✤ Set up a see-saw like this.

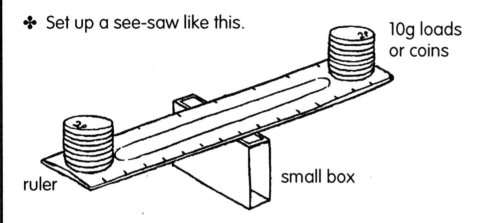

10g loads or coins

ruler

small box

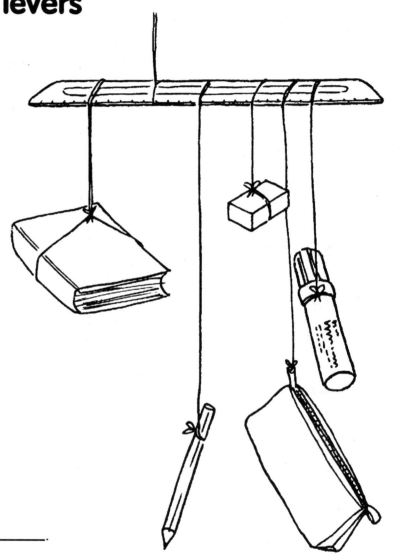

✤ Can you make it balance:
• with the same load on each side;
• with unequal loads on each side;
• with no loads on one side?
What did you find out?

✤ Complete this sentence:
• To make a see-saw (lever) balance with different loads on each side the heavier load needs to be

_____

✤ Use what you have found out to design and make a mobile display.

Name _____

Dino-jaws

✤ Copy or trace these shapes on to card, then cut them out.

✤ Punch holes, as shown, and join the matching parts (A–A and B–B) together with paper fasteners.

B ● ✤ Glue guide over this strip so it is free to move.

↔

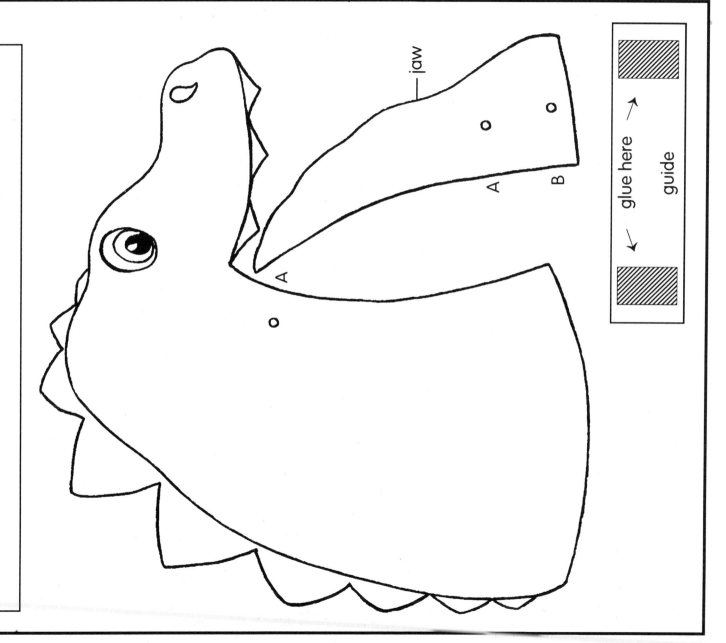

jaw

A

B

A

glue here

guide

Name _____

Linkages

Wavy Ted

✿ Copy or trace these shapes on to card. Cut them out and colour them.

✿ Punch holes and use glue and two paper fasteners to join Ted together.

B ● ✿ Glue guide over this strip so it is free to move.

⟷

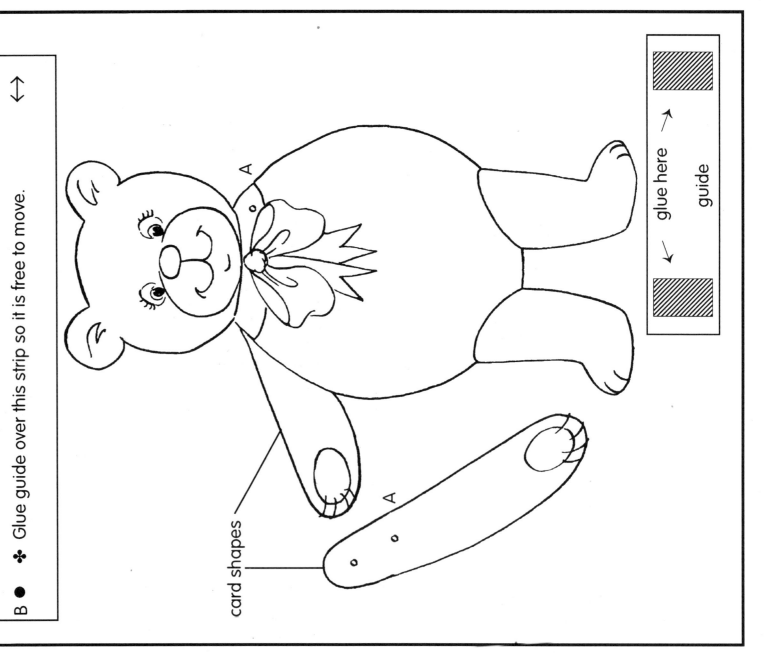

A

A

card shapes

← glue here →

guide

Name _____

Ear Ear

✤ Copy or trace these shapes on to card. Cut them out and colour them.

✤ Punch holes, and use glue and three paper fasteners to make the rabbit.

✤ Make him wave his ears!

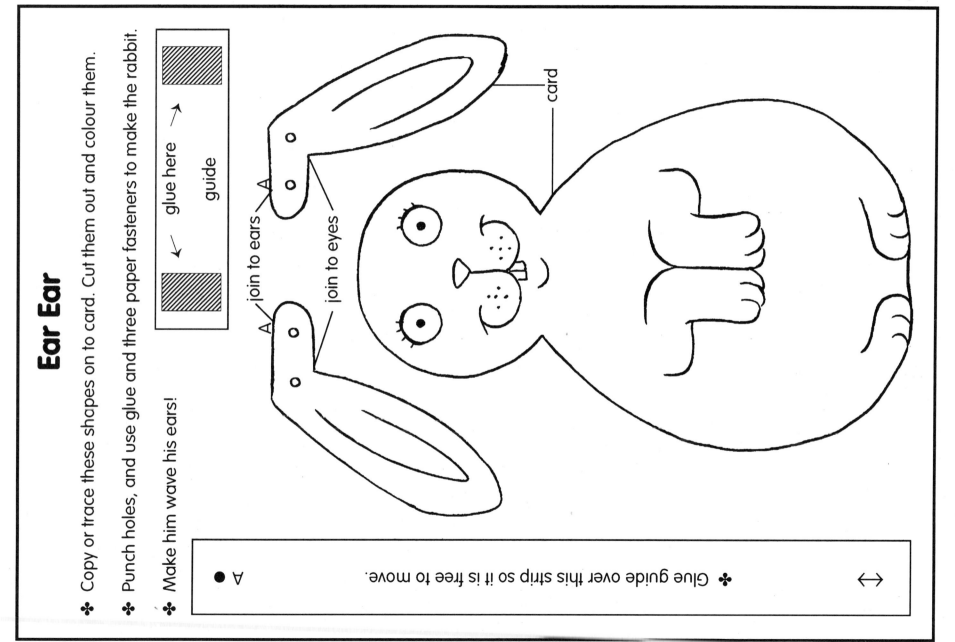

glue here →

guide

← glue here

join to ears

A

join to eyes

A

join to eyes

A

join to ears

card

✤ Glue guide over this strip so it is free to move.

A ●

↔

Name _____

Linkages

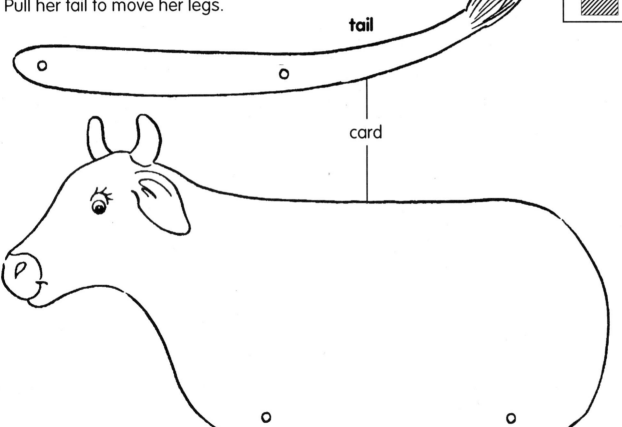

Moo-ve it!

♣ Copy or trace the parts of the cow on to card. Cut them out and colour them in.

♣ Link her parts with four paper fasteners.

♣ Pull her tail to move her legs.

tail

card

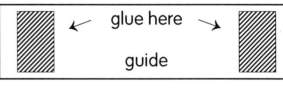

← glue here →

guide

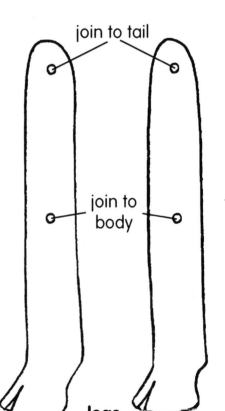

join to tail

join to body

legs

Name _____

Cocky locky

❖ Copy or trace these shapes on to card.

❖ Cut them out carefully.

❖ Punch holes where shown.

❖ Join A–A, and so on, with paper fastener joints.

glue here →

← guide

top of beak

lower beak

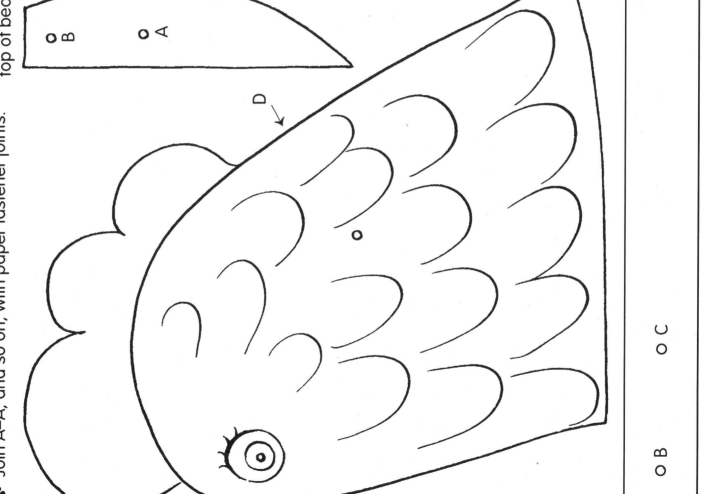

B ○

C ○

Pulleys

Name _____

Pulley investigations

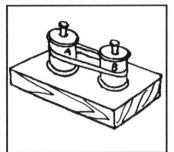

A pulley is a wheel with a groove. It can be used to drive other pulleys using a belt or a band.

✣ Look at these two pulleys

• Which way will B turn if you turn A clockwise here?

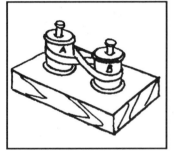

• What about this one?

✣ Try using more pulleys. Can you make pulley B go a different way from the other two?

✣ Try using different-sized pulleys. What happens?

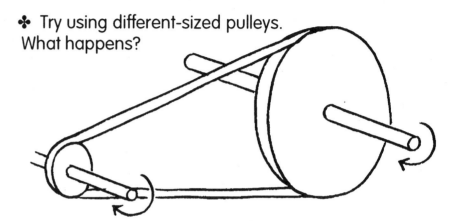

✣ Try using pulleys to drive a model, like this roundabout.

lolly stick joined to reel with Blu-Tack.

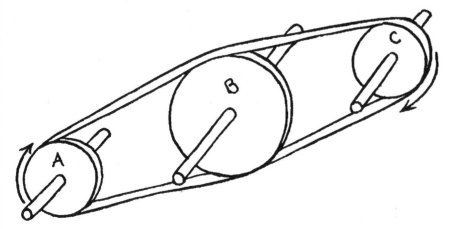

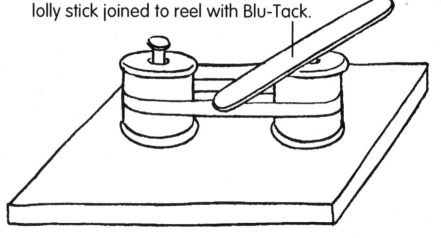

Name _____

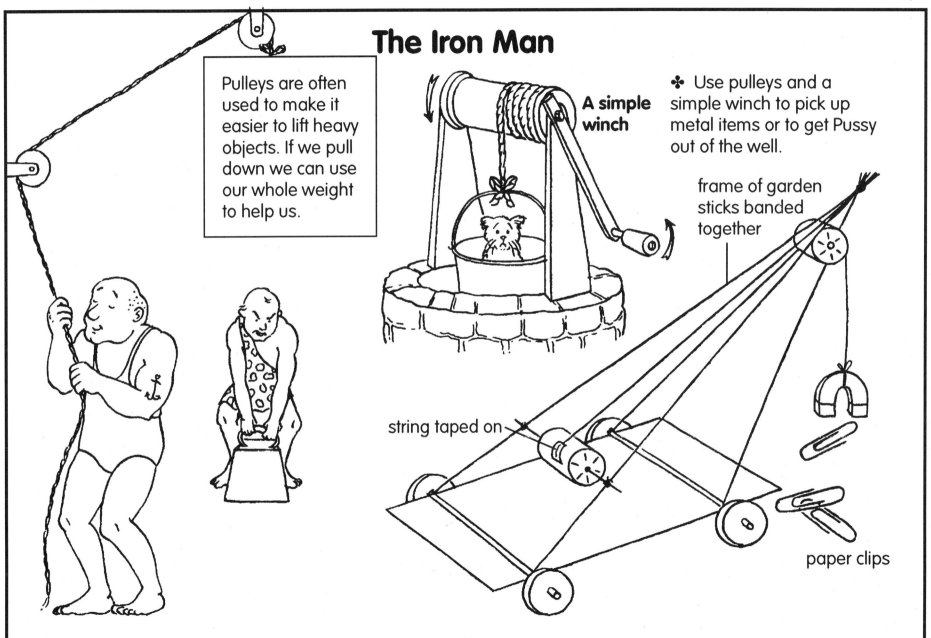

The Iron Man

Pulleys are often used to make it easier to lift heavy objects. If we pull down we can use our whole weight to help us.

A simple winch

✤ Use pulleys and a simple winch to pick up metal items or to get Pussy out of the well.

frame of garden sticks banded together

string taped on

paper clips

Name _____

Pulleys

Conveyors and tracked vehicles

Pulleys can be used to drive a conveyor belt or a tracked vehicle.

❖ Try one of these two ideas.

❖ Now design and make something which uses a conveyor belt or caterpillar tracks.

Conveyor belt

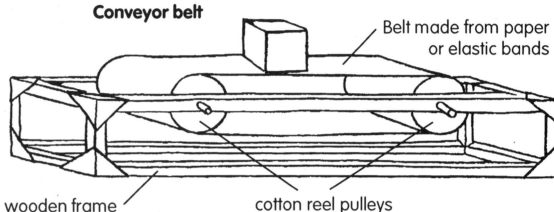

Belt made from paper or elastic bands

wooden frame

cotton reel pulleys

Track driven vehicle

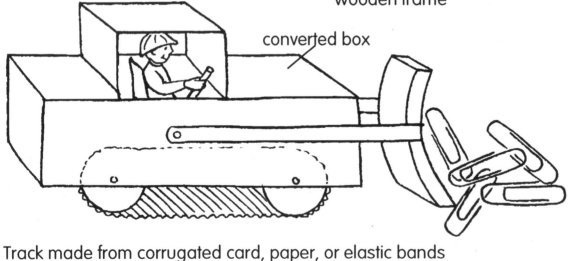

converted box

Track made from corrugated card, paper, or elastic bands

❖ Draw your design on the back of this sheet.

Using a motor

Pulleys are often used to transfer the drive from an electric motor to a model. The small pulley on the motor rotates very quickly but only turns the large pulley slowly. This is called **gearing down**.

When a small pulley drives a larger one there is an increased turning effect or **torque**. The large pulley is able to move heavier loads.

card disc

plywood wheel

belt and pulley

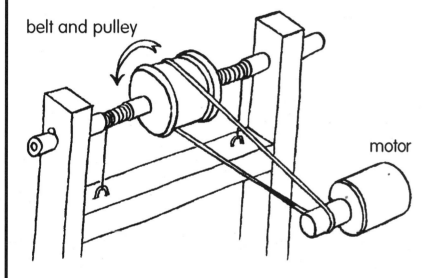

motor

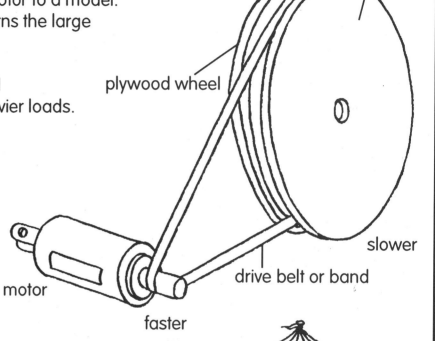

motor

faster

slower

drive belt or band

Pulleys can also be used to transfer movement from electric motors.

❧ Design and make a motorised model using a pulley drive system. Here are two ideas to help you – a roundabout and a lifting gate mechanism.

❧ Sketch your design on the back of this sheet.

Name _____

Gears

Investigations on gears

❖ Make a collection of pictures of objects which use gears. What do the gears look like?

❖ Add arrows to the pictures below to show how they work.

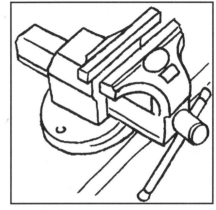
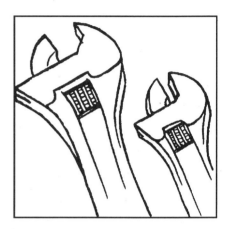

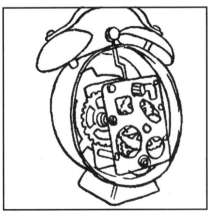
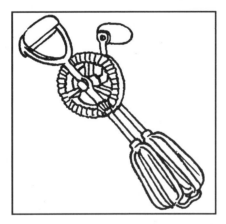
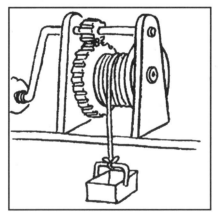

❖ On the back of this sheet make an accurate labelled drawing of something that uses gears, and explain what the gears do.

Using gears

✤ Use the gears from a construction kit to set up these gear systems.

✤ Then answer the questions below.

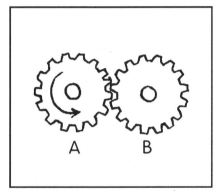

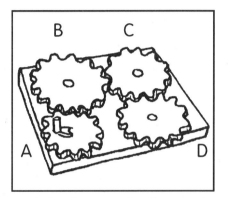

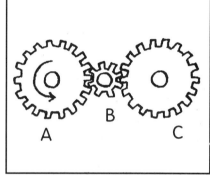

• Which way do these turn? Which gear is faster?

• Which way do these turn? Which gear is fastest?

• What happens when a small gear drives a larger one?

• Which way do the gears turn? Which gear is fastest?

• What happens when you turn: gear A; gear B? Which gear is easier to stop?

✤ Now use the construction kit gears to make a working model such as a crane, a lifting barrier or a vehicle.

When a small gear drives a larger one it can move heavier loads.
This is called gearing down.

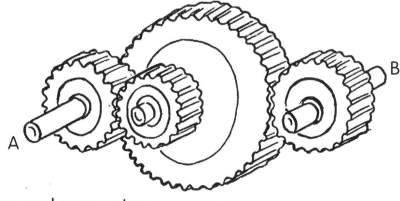

compound gear system

Gears

Name the gear

❧ Try to find an example of at least four of these gears either in a kit or a simple machine.

• How do they work?

• What are they used for?

❧ Use some of them to build a model.

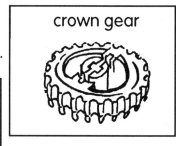

crown gear

rack (often used with spur gears)

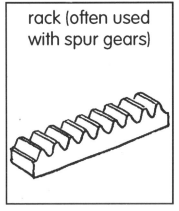

spur gears

ratchet

pawl

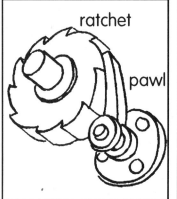

pinion

rack

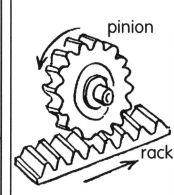

worm gear

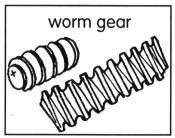

Types of gear

chain drive

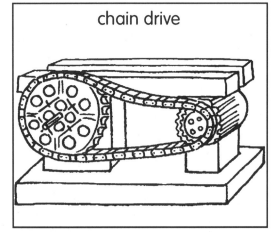

bevel gears

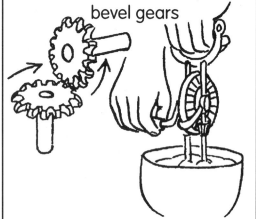

gearshaft crown gear pinion

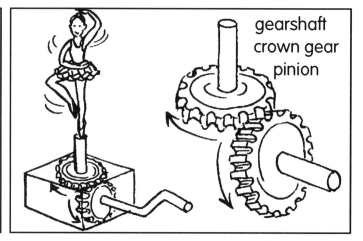

Making your own gears

❖ Try out some of these ideas.

❖ Then design and make a model using your own gears.

Elastic bands wrapped around cotton reels

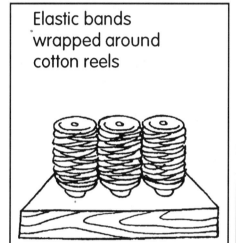

Corrugated card wrapped around tins or other cylindrical containers

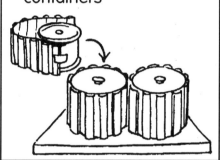

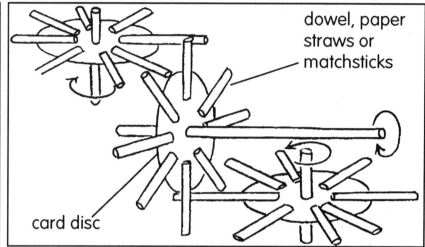

dowel, paper straws or matchsticks

card disc

square wood (8 or 10mm cross section)

matchstick or dowel gear teeth

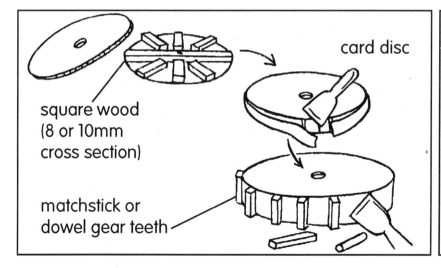

card disc

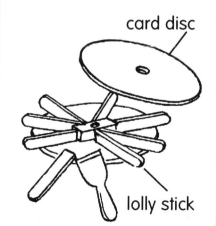

card disc

lolly stick

Bought gear wheels can be used with axles made from wooden dowel

The Aztec calendar: 1

The Aztecs were skilful astronomers who studied the movements of the sun, stars and planets. They worked out a solar calendar of 365 days, but they also used a sacred calendar of 260 days to calculate the date of religious festivals and to foretell the future.

✤ Look at page 107.

The wheel on the right represents the solar calendar which was for everyday use. There were 18 months of 20 days, plus 5 extra days which were thought to be unlucky. The wheel on the left represents the sacred calendar which was divided into 20 periods of 13 days.

Once every 52 years the sacred year ended at the same time as the calendar year. When this happened the Aztecs feared that the world would end. That night all the people would watch to see whether the sky went on revolving.
All fires had to be put out; all pots were destroyed.

The priests began a ceremony to bring about a new period of history. They offered sacrifices to the gods and turned their sacred fire-sticks in the holes of a wooden board to start a new fire.

As soon as the priests had lit the new fire, runners with torches carried it to all parts of the valley of Mexico.
When the sun rose again the people believed it was because of the power of the priests' rituals that life could go on. All fires were rekindled and new pots were made.
The last Aztec Festival of the New Fire took place in 1507.

Name _____

The Aztec calendar: 2

♣ Cut out the two card circles.

♣ Punch holes through the two central dots.

♣ Glue matchsticks round the edge of each circle on the marked lines.

♣ Attach the circles to a background card using paper fasteners.

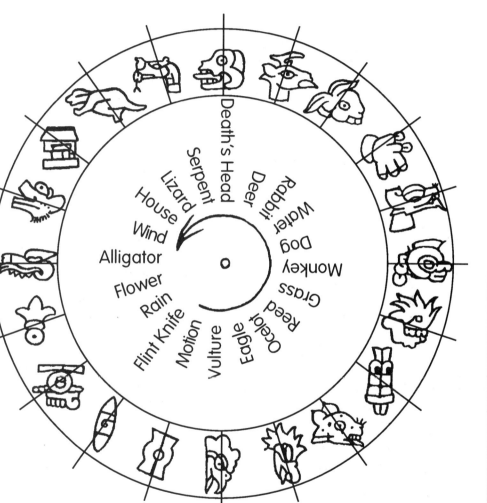

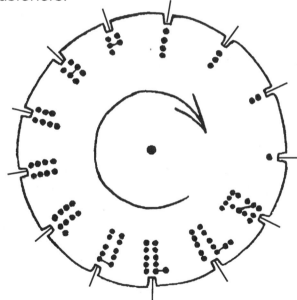

♣ How many times do you have to turn the big wheel before both wheels are back in the start position?

Pneumatics and hydraulics

Name _____

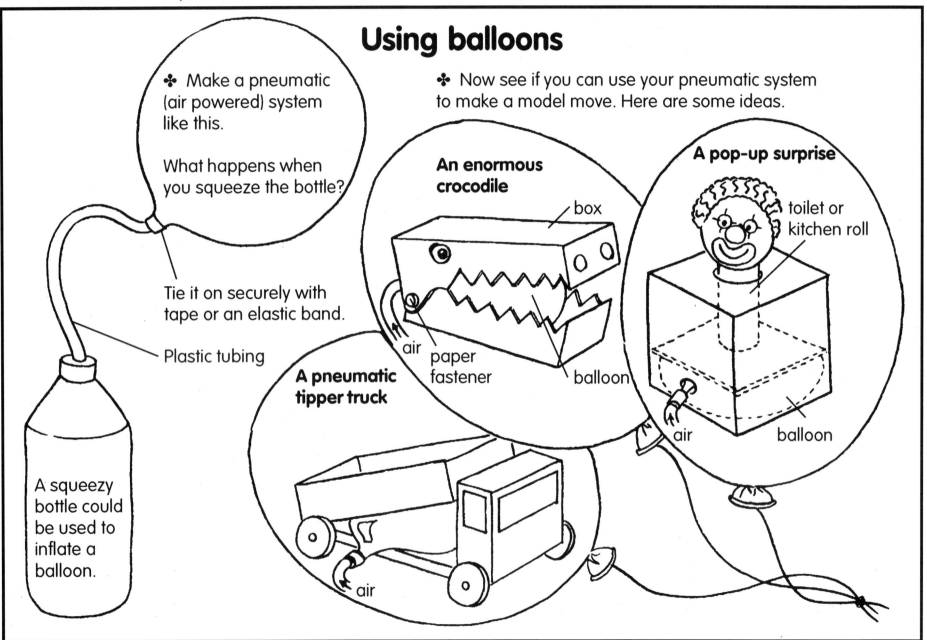

Using balloons

❖ Make a pneumatic (air powered) system like this.

What happens when you squeeze the bottle?

Tie it on securely with tape or an elastic band.

Plastic tubing

A squeezy bottle could be used to inflate a balloon.

❖ Now see if you can use your pneumatic system to make a model move. Here are some ideas.

An enormous crocodile

box

air paper fastener balloon

A pop-up surprise

toilet or kitchen roll

air balloon

A pneumatic tipper truck

air

Using syringes

❖ Join two plastic disposable syringes like this.

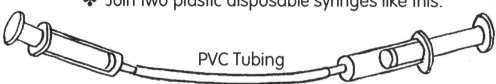

PVC Tubing

What happens when you push one plunger in? Does it make any difference if you use different-sized syringes?

❖ Use this idea to make a pneumatically operated model like the examples shown on this page.

A pop-up ghost

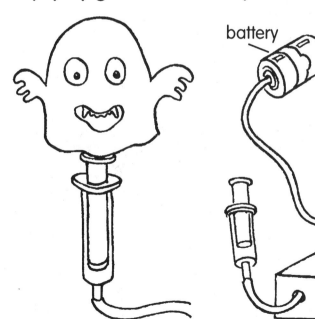

A pneumatic switch

buzzer

battery

foam
spring

foil-type
switch

Syringes can be
hidden in boxes

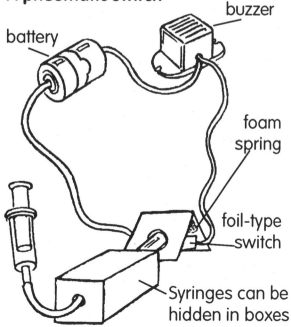

A pneumatic cat lift

This side will need
to be heavier

paper fastener
attached loosely.

string

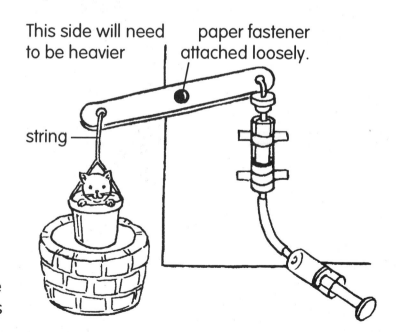

N.B. Please remember there are labels that sit next to the
two larger diagrams and these have roughly been placed.

Pneumatics and hydraulics

Name _____

Hydraulics

✤ Half-fill two syringes with water in a bowl.

✤ Turn them upside down, tap them and squeeze any air bubbles out.

✤ Join them together with a water-filled tube.

✤ Try pushing or pulling water from one to another.

✤ Use hydraulics to make a model move. Here are some ideas.

A hydraulic lifting device

A hydraulic digger

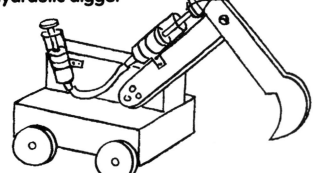

Use a construction kit.

Cammy the duck

♣ Copy or trace these shapes on to card and cut them out.

♣ Punch holes where shown.

♣ Glue Cammy's head on to the lever strip (position it first with Blu-Tack).

♣ Join A-A and B-B with loose paper fastener joints.

Cam

○ A

● Fit paper fastener handle here.

♣ Wind the handle and watch Cammy nod.

♣ Try using cam mechanisms to make other models move.

glue this end

Score along here and fold

Lever strip – rest folded edge on the cam

Weight the end of this with Plasticine or Blu-Tack

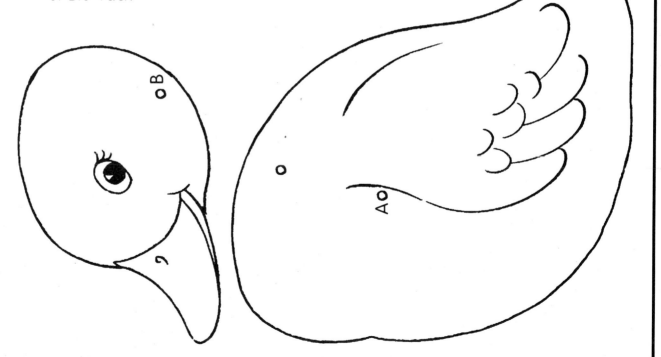

Name _____

Cams and cranks

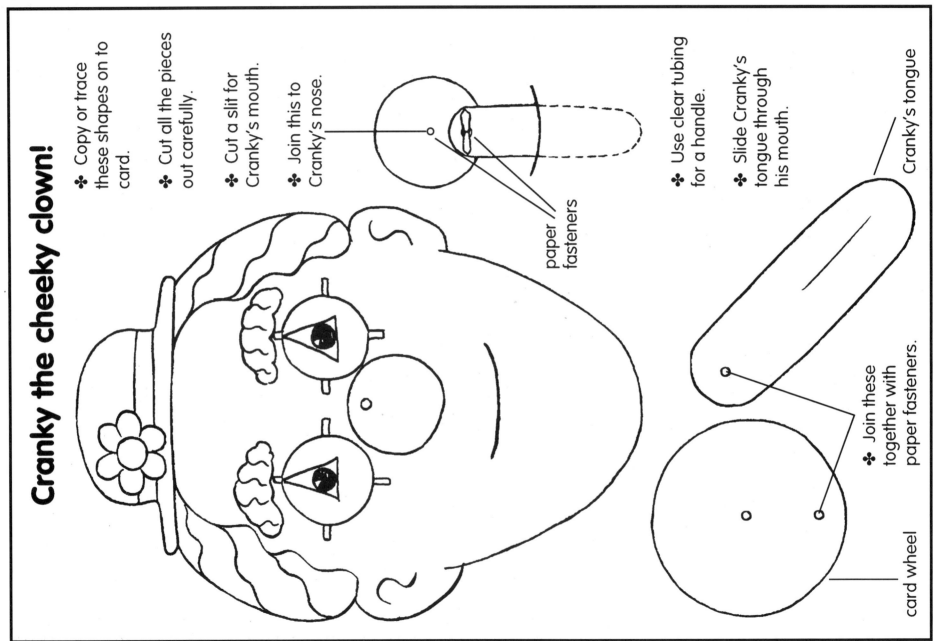

Cranky the cheeky clown!

✿ Copy or trace these shapes on to card.

✿ Cut all the pieces out carefully.

✿ Cut a slit for Cranky's mouth.

✿ Join this to Cranky's nose.

paper fasteners

✿ Use clear tubing for a handle.

✿ Slide Cranky's tongue through his mouth.

Cranky's tongue

✿ Join these together with paper fasteners.

card wheel

Furry Ferdinand

Fold over
and glue

Score and fold

✦ Fold and stick the edges of this sheet to form a tray.

✦ Put some iron filings in the tray and move them, using a magnet under the tray, to give Ferdinand hair, whiskers or a beard.

Score and fold

Magnets

Name _____

Island boat race

✤ Cut out these sailing boats.

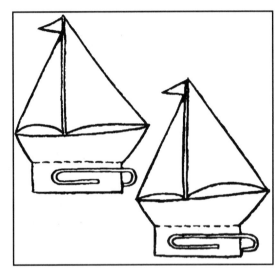

✤ Fold each one along the dotted line and attach a paper clip to the flap.

✤ Now glue the island, and the water around it, on to a thin sheet of card.

✤ Use magnets underneath to see which boat is the first to sail right round the island.

Electrical toys and games

✤ Make a collection of electrical toys and games.

✤ Choose your favourite, sketch it carefully below and explain how it works.

Here is one idea you could try – a game for a steady hand!

from a power supply

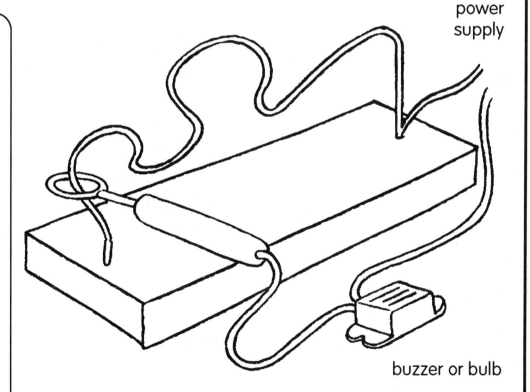

buzzer or bulb

✤ Now design and make your own electrical toy.

Name _____

Investigating a torch

♣ Make a clear labelled drawing of a torch.

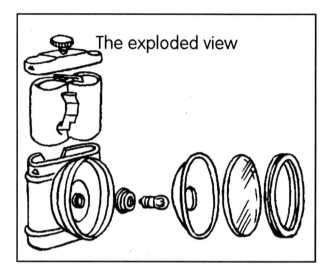

The exploded view

♣ Carefully take it apart, draw all the different pieces and say what they are for.

♣ Now put it back together again. Does it still work?

Technology tool box

Sarah's tool box has got into a mess.

♣ Can you help her find her missing tools in the grid below?

They are written backwards, across, down and diagonally.

Sarah's tools	glasspaper	ruler
hand drill	nails	pencil
hammer	screws	hacksaw
screwdriver	glue spreader	g clamp
vice	scissors	snips
hole punch	paintbrush	drill bits
glue	paint	bench hook

```
t  h  r  e  u  l  g  x  y  p  a  i  n  t  b  r  u  s  h  f  d
k  o  o  h  h  c  n  e  b  m  s  u  h  a  m  r  e  d  j  l  c
h  l  j  s  c  r  e  w  s  e  n  a  t  t  e  f  x  j  n  m  l
l  e  p  n  o  q  s  w  j  n  i  k  v  d  n  g  p  z  r  q  r
j  p  a  i  n  t  a  l  i  h  p  x  a  u  x  f  e  o  u  u  e
s  u  a  e  p  s  h  y  a  x  s  e  l  j  m  n  o  p  l  p  v
t  n  m  z  k  v  t  n  o  t  r  t  h  s  h  a  m  m  e  r  i
i  c  t  c  g  w  d  p  o  p  s  s  e  r  q  i  q  u  r  u  r
b  h  a  m  x  d  z  t  s  z  p  e  n  c  i  l  h  k  p  i  d
l  h  b  w  r  w  r  e  j  j  w  v  m  s  f  s  f  g  m  f  w
l  z  n  i  r  e  u  j  r  e  c  i  v  f  l  x  y  o  a  z  e
i  k  l  t  o  l  s  k  d  s  r  o  s  s  i  c  s  c  l  b  r
r  l  f  w  g  c  l  b  s  g  e  w  p  t  d  m  w  r  c  j  c
d  r  g  t  j  x  a  g  l  a  s  s  p  a  p  e  r  a  g  x  s
```

♣ Try designing your own word search on squared paper.   How will you make it look special?

Name _____

Vocabulary

Technology jumblies

Here are some technological words which have got jumbled up.

♣ Write them correctly.

♣ Draw an example of each one and say what it does.

yellup = _____

rage = _____

lesax = _____

veerl = _____

inglkae = _____

itwsch = _____

♣ Now design your own technology word puzzle.

Adventure World

Adventure World need some help to launch their new theme park.

✤ Develop **one** of the ideas below:

1   Design some new advertising materials for the theme park, such as posters or leaflets. Why not add a pop-up section or some movement using linkages? Sketch and label your favourite design on the back of this sheet.

2   Model a new scene for the Ghost Train (this could be done in an old cardboard box). How could you make it **really** scary?

3   Think up some new promotional items to give to visitors. These should be relatively cheap to produce in quantity, such as sun or rain hats, zany card sunglasses or pin badges. Sketch your two best ideas on the back of this sheet.

4   Design and make a model of a new ride for the park. It could have moving parts, lights and may even be computer controlled. (Use construction kit parts or other materials if you wish.)

Name _____

Assessment

Castaway

You have been shipwrecked on a desert island. You have managed to build a rough shelter and have found a well with a supply of fresh water. You are living on a diet of fruit, nuts and raw fish.

When searching the island you came upon an abandoned camp from a wartime occupation. You have found a number of items which you think will be useful.

♣ Devise one of the following, using only the supplies you have found.

1 A lighting system for the shelter.

2 An alarm to protect your food-store from marauding monkeys.

3 A motorised labour-saving device such as air-conditioning for the shelter, a powered winch for the well or possibly a simple washing-machine.

Your supplies

several batteries	cardboard
some wire	elastic bands
a few bulbs	foil
sticky tape	some small metal strips
clothes pegs	bell
drawing pins	buzzer
paper clips	a small motor
some scraps of wood	some simple machine parts
paper fasteners	basic constructional materials

Crossing the island

You have been invited to join an expedition to explore an uninhabited island.

Your job is to plan the trip and decide what items of equipment you will need.

One of the many problems the expedition will face is that there are no roads on the island. In order to explore it thoroughly you will need to cross difficult and dangerous terrain.

✤ Design and make a model of a type of vehicle that could transport both passengers and equipment.

Your solution could include a motor, light or a buzzer. If time allows you could control your vehicle using the computer.

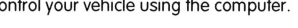

Name _____

Planning sheets

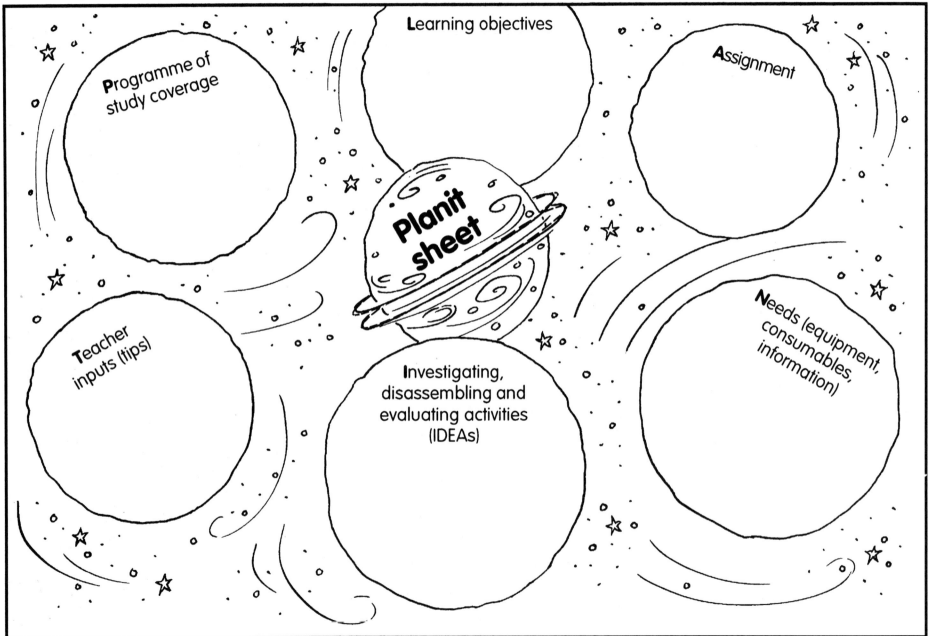

Learning objectives

Programme of study coverage

Assignment

Planit sheet

Teacher inputs (tips)

Investigating, disassembling and evaluating activities (IDEAs)

Needs (equipment, consumables, information)

Name _____

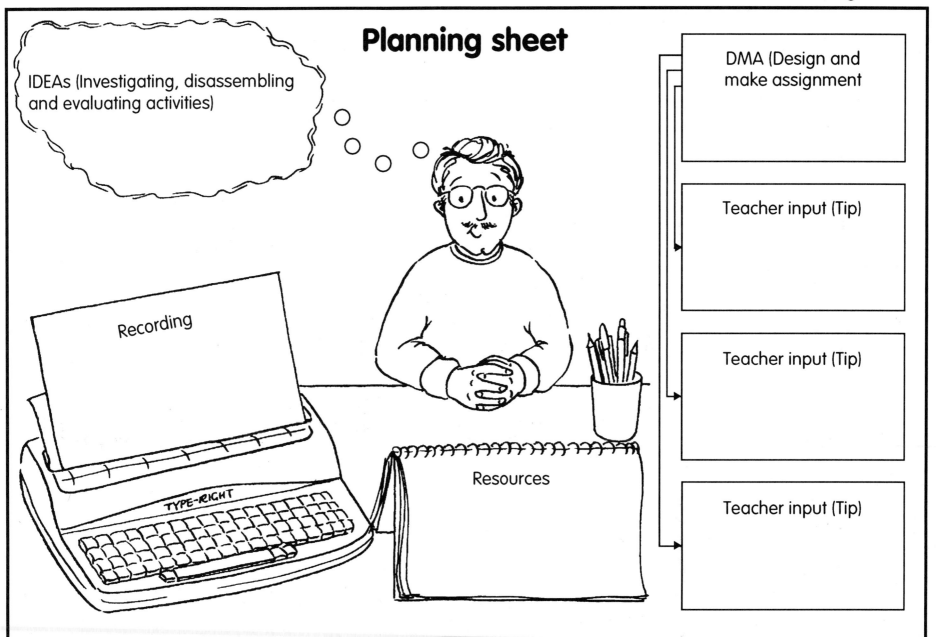

Planning sheet

IDEAs (Investigating, disassembling and evaluating activities)

Recording

Resources

TYPE-RIGHT

DMA (Design and make assignment

Teacher input (Tip)

Teacher input (Tip)

Teacher input (Tip)

Name _____

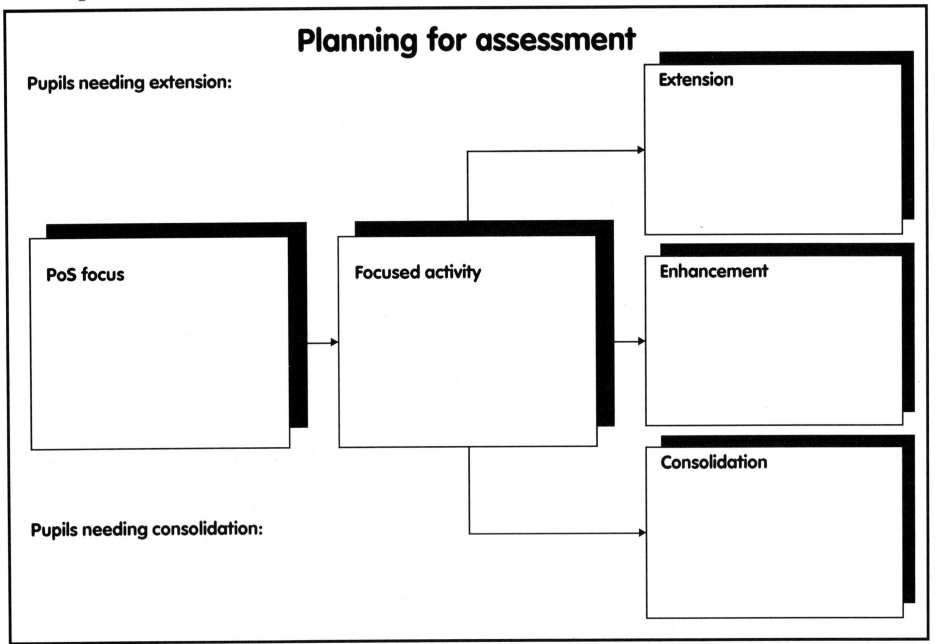

Planning for assessment

Pupils needing extension:

Extension

PoS focus

Focused activity

Enhancement

Consolidation

Pupils needing consolidation:

3D drawings

❖ Sketch a small box in three dimensions. Use faint lines.

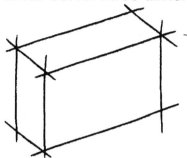

Don't worry if lines overshoot. They can be rubbed out afterwards.

Isometric paper under your drawing sheet will help. Keep it in place with Blu-Tack.

❖ Now try to sketch the box in different positions.

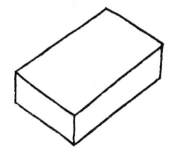 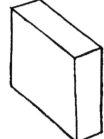 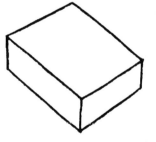 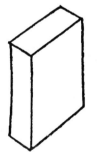

❖ Practise drawing different boxes.

❖ Add shading.

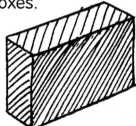

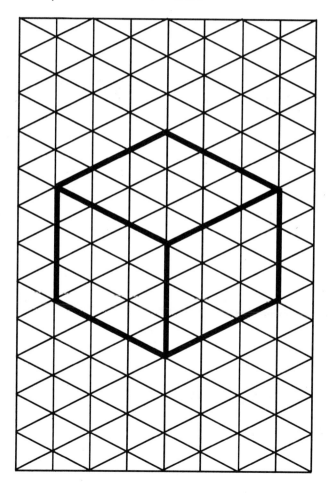

Graphics

Shading and texture

Careful shading in sketches can help to show the textures of different materials.

Here are some useful tips.

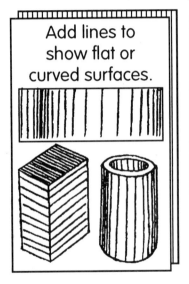

Add lines to show flat or curved surfaces.

Dots or lines at various angles can indicate fabric.

Use solid shading to show areas in shadow.

Draw in lines to show woodgrain.

Faint diagonal lines represent shiny or see-through materials.

✤ Use some of the above techniques to show the textures of the materials used in these objects.

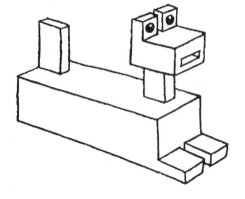

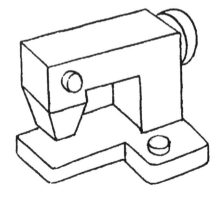

Light and shadow

Shading can be used on drawings to indicate shadow.

✤ Practise shading these objects.

✤ On each one draw an arrow to show in which direction the light is coming from.

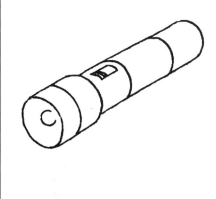
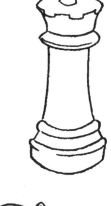

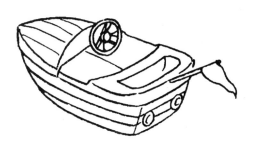

Name _____

One point perspective

Perspective drawing takes into account the idea that lines appear to get closer and they actually appear to meet in the distance. You can see this effect if you look along a long building or straight road.

The place where the lines appear to meet is called the **vanishing point** (VP).

There are three stages in drawing an object in single point perspective.

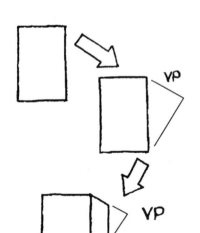

1 Draw the front of the object.

2 Draw faint lines to the vanishing point (VP).

3 Complete the outline of the object, and remove the faint lines to the vanishing point.

EYE LEVEL   VP

✤ Try drawing some simple boxes in one point perspective.

Two point perspective

If you can use two vanishing points in your drawing it will look even more realistic.

Regard the cube as the basic building block.
❖ Draw as many as you can.
❖ Draw the cubes again and turn them into hollow cubes.
❖ Fill your sheet of paper.

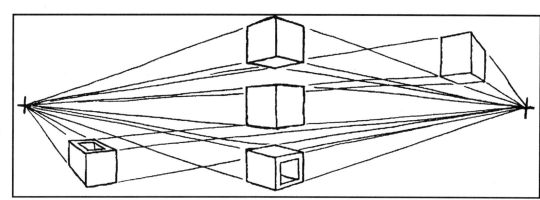

Worm's eye view (this gives the impression of looking up at an object).

Eye level

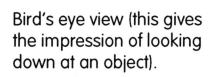

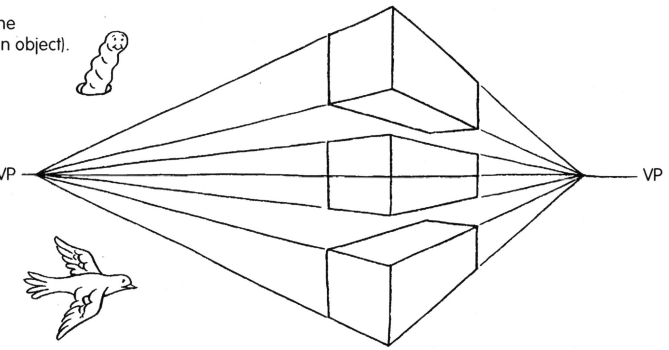

VP   VP

Bird's eye view (this gives the impression of looking down at an object).

Name _____

Graphics

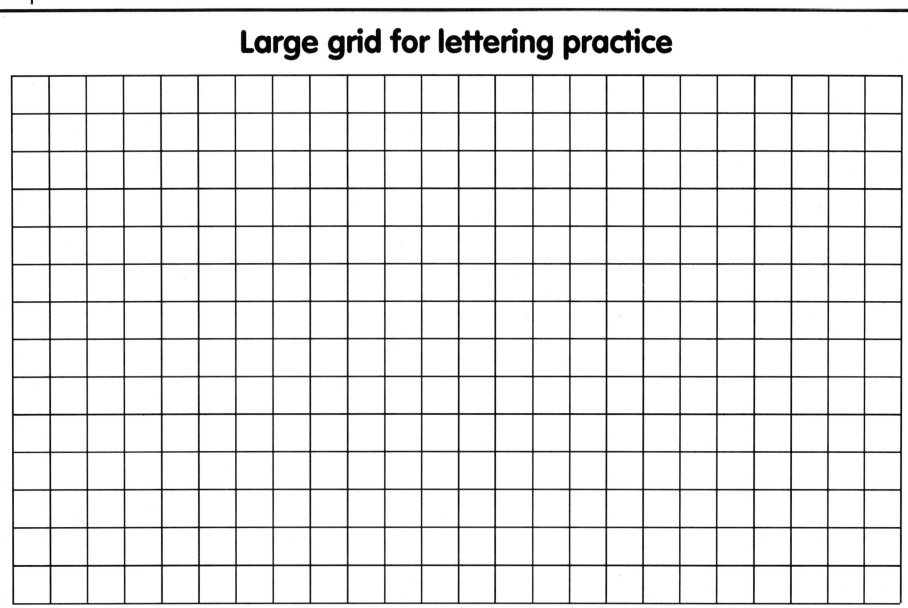

Large grid for lettering practice

Small grid for lettering practice

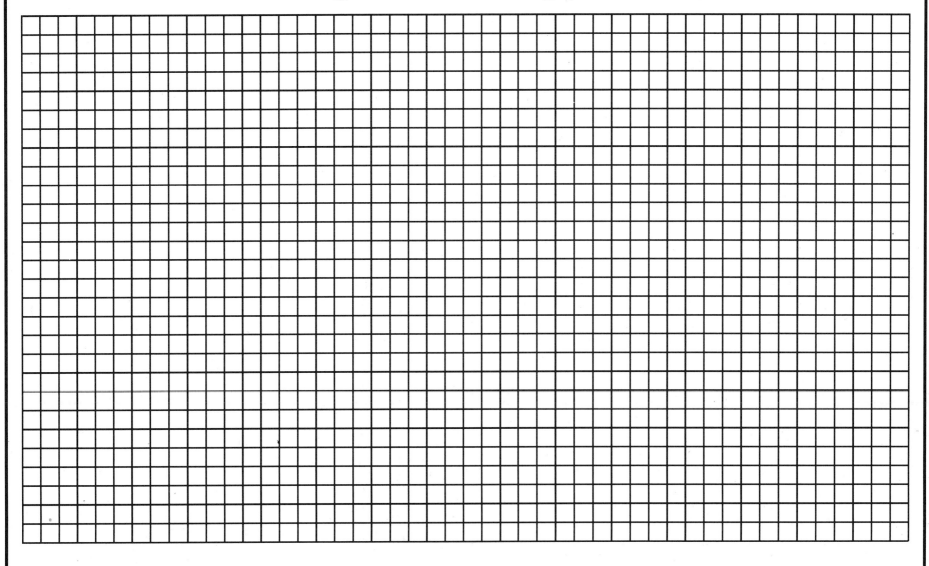

Graphics

Name _____

Grid for drawing 3D views

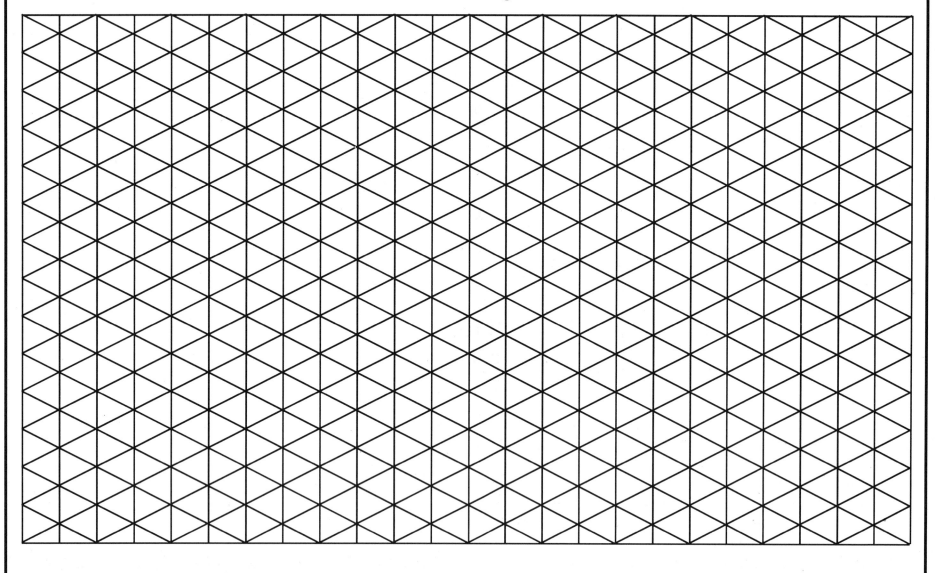

Design and technology project

Suggestions for improvements to my work:

Name   Date

My project is to:

To be successful I will need to consider:

Children's design sheets

Name _____

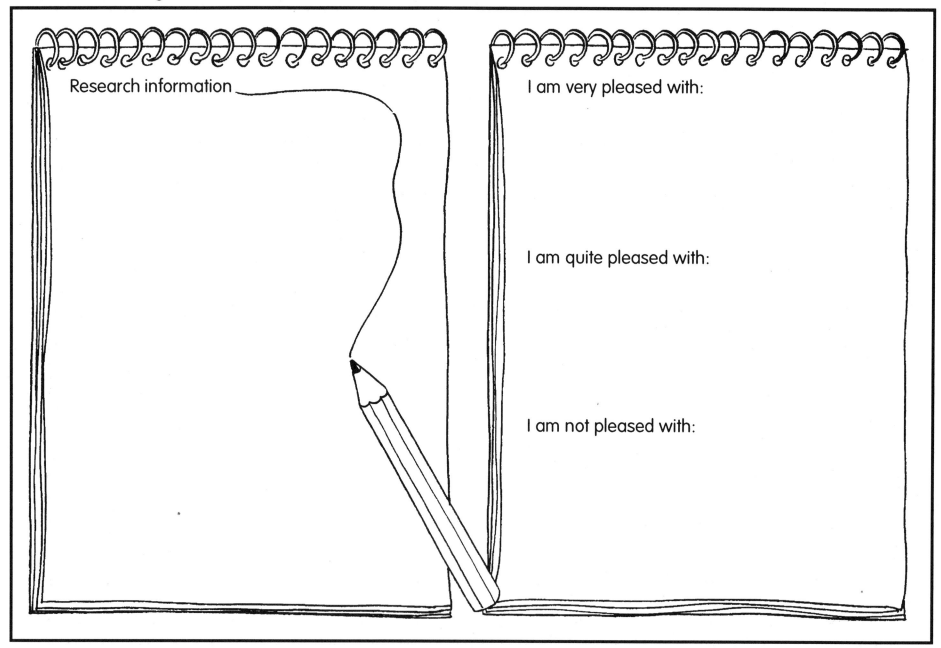

Research information

I am very pleased with:

I am quite pleased with:

I am not pleased with:

Name _____

How I did it:

My ideas:

Children's design sheets

Name _____

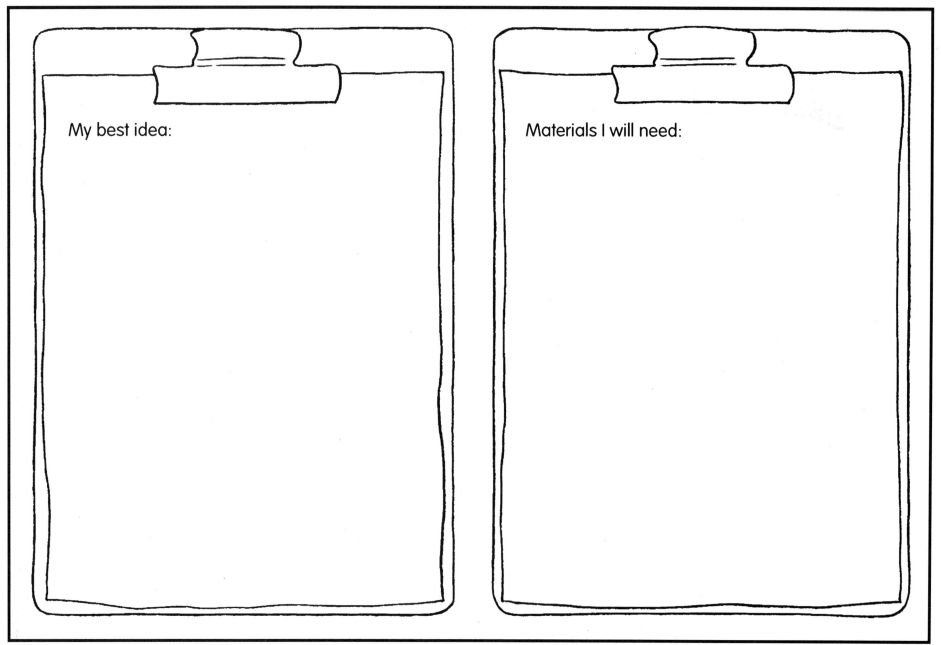

My best idea:

Materials I will need:

Evidence sample sheet

Date:

Pupil/s involved:

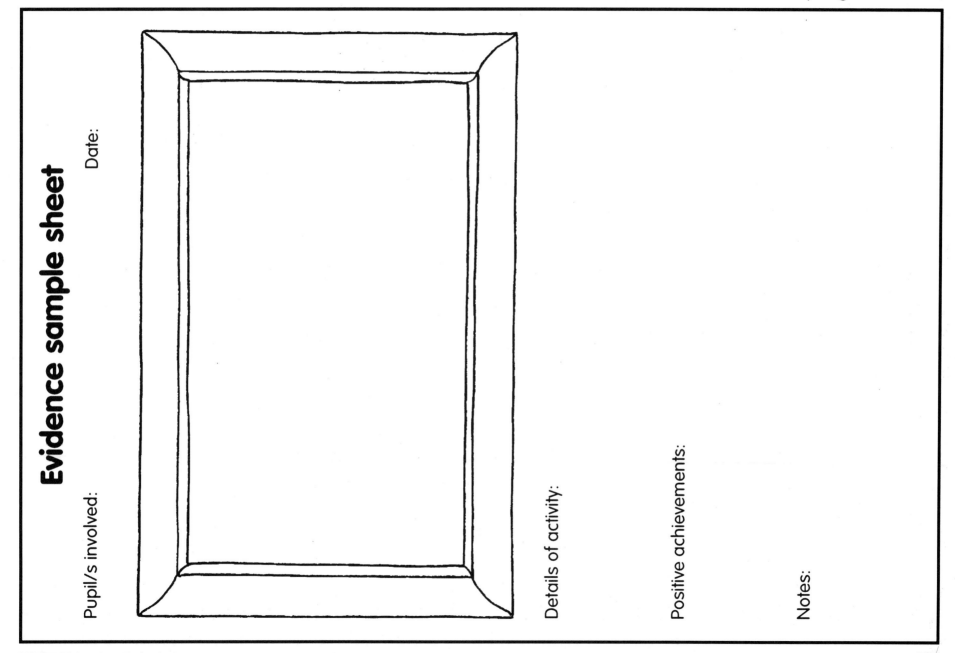

Details of activity:

Positive achievements:

Notes:

Name _____

Disassembly/evaluation

Ideas sheet: 1

Investigating, Disassembling and Evaluating Activities

Name	Date		
Drawing of a		What it does	Things I like about it
			How it could be improved

Ideas sheet: 2

A good _____ needs the following features:	5 star rating	Comments and suggested improvements
•		
•		
•		
•		
•		
•		

Investigating, Disassembling and Evaluating Activities

Name	Date

Type of product:

What does it do?

Any other information:

Disassembly/evaluation

Name _____

Labelled drawing of the product being investigated	Exploded diagram showing all the different parts

Progress review sheet

Pupil details

Date	Comments						'Best fit' level at end of Key Stage:
	Interest and motivation in designing and making:	Ability to use materials and equipment safely:	Ability to communicate design ideas and explain the purpose of what they are doing:	Knowledge of a variety of materials, tools and equipment:	Understanding of simple mechanisms and structures:	Other comments (this could include a list of the D&T activities carried out):	AT1 Designing 1 2 3 4 5
							AT2 Making 1 2 3 4 5
							(circle most appropriate)

Appeal for resources

Name _____

Technology resources needed

We need: _____

_____

If you can help, please bring or send any to:

_____

in class _____

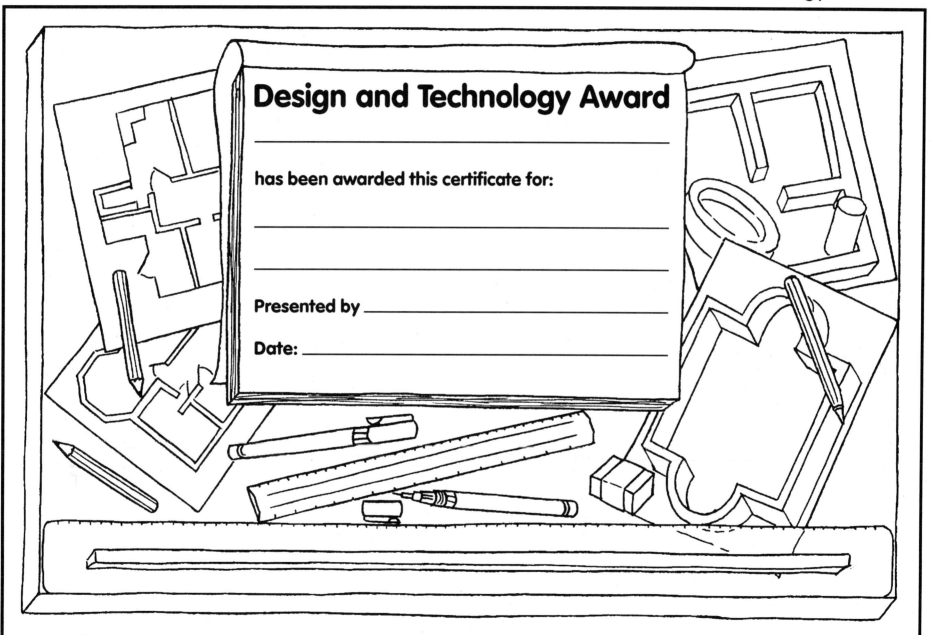

Design and Technology Award

_____

has been awarded this certificate for:

_____

_____

Presented by _____

Date: _____

Permission letter

Parental permission letter for food activities

_____ School

Dear Parent/Guardian

During the course of food activities to be carried out in school your child may need to taste certain items of food. Please let us know if your child has any special dietary requirements which could prevent him/her from tasting certain foods. I would be grateful if you could complete the form below and return it to your child's class teacher for our records.

With thanks for your co-operation.

Headteacher

I give permission for _____
(name of child) to take part in food activities which form an essential part of the school curriculum.

She/He (please cross out whichever line does not apply)
(a) can eat a variety of foods.
(b) should not eat the following foods: _____

Other comments _____

Signed _____ Date _____
Parent/Guardian